Fishing

A Trout Stream and a Way of Life

By Mike Reuther

"A trout is a moment of beauty known only to those who seek it." - Arnold Gingrich

This book is dedicated to all the crazy fly fishers out there.

Chapter 1

      Jack McAllister knew every hatch on every trout stream of Central Pennsylvania. Much of his life revolved around casting dry flies, wet flies, nymphs and other food imitations at that elusive creature known as the trout. He would have it no other way. Jack had gained a reputation as one of the most respected fly fisherman in the state, a dubious distinction in that it gained him no great rewards or wide renown other than that realized in fly-fishing circles.

His had been a mostly quiet life—a true trout bum's existence—one of fishing, guiding and tying flies. In Jack's mind, nothing was finer than catching an evening hatch down at the Shad River, just before dusk, when the trout were rising. Jack built this life for himself, an unhurried and quiet existence in this remote mountain area where the living was easy, and a man's word was as good as a handshake. But it all changed in the year of the Great Green Drake Hatch.

In the years before the arrival of the Great Green Drake Hatch, when Memorial Day weekend in the Green Spring Valley was nothing more than a camper's holiday and many a fly fisherman would have been hard put to find the Shad on the map, things had been different. In those days, Jack's home was a ramshackle cabin just a long cast from the Shad. He had lived well there, perhaps even somewhat happily, or at least in a state that didn't approach anything that could be even remotely referred to as misery.

Happiness, as Jack liked to say, was a damn elusive proposition, but with proper planning, you could latch onto it, and then "hold on like hell" as if you're hooking up with one of the Shad River's healthy sized Brown Trout.

"Hell, even if it breaks your damn line, you can have yourself a nice ride," Jack had said more than once to Max Soothsayer.

Soothsayer nodded and smiled as he gazed out toward the water.

Jack and Soothsayer had spent countless hours together wading the pools of the Shad and the other streams feeding into it. Soothsayer was getting along in years now, and didn't head out to fish as much as he had in his younger days. A bum knee forced him to use a wading staff even in the calmest stretches of water. Most of his time was spent tying flies in the back of the Roll Cast, the general store off Route 6 he owned, where Jack dropped in nearly every day for a sandwich, to meet a client needing guiding, or for the latest gossip. Although it was in truth a store, it was also part barroom, part eatery and more or less the social center of the village, that is, if you could call the half-dozen homes clustered nearby along Route 6 a village of any kind. Many of the homes were summer cottages, used by hunters or trout fishermen who could be depended upon to show up at the Shad every spring.

Soothsayer was one of the few people Jack could stand to be around for any stretch of time. For one thing, Soothsayer had more knowledge about the Shad River hatches than anyone he knew. Soothsayer also had a keen sense of just what the fish would take. More than once Jack had come tromping into Soothsayer's store in his waders, frustrated over a particularly troublesome hatch the trout were feeding ravenously upon, but which were ignoring his every cast. Soothsayer, always calm in a crisis, would make a few simple suggestions, or perhaps calmly trim the hackles off some of Jack's flies before sending him back out to the water. Often, Soothsayer's sage advice turned around what had been a horrible fishing day.

It was true that Jack loved to fish so passionately that he was thought to be a little off his nut by the local folks. Indeed, he was obsessed with the whole business of catching trout. Jack was never able to explain this fever or love affair or whatever the hell it was he had with fly fishing, but he didn't have much time for folks who elevated fly fishing to art or religion or other nonsense either. Damn it. He just liked to fish. Being out on the water with a fly rod when the trout were surfacing to grab white mayflies or March Browns or sulphurs. Well … there was just no better time to be alive as far as Jack was concerned.

He'd fished the Shad and every one of its feeder streams from Green Spring Valley to the New York state line. And if there was any prettier stretch of God's lush landscape or any more productive trout water in America than that fifty-mile swath of terrain, he'd be damned if he knew where it was.

He'd been on some of those legendary trout streams out West and wet his line on more than a few of the other rivers famous for big brown trout, in the Adirondacks and up through Vermont. He took trips every August out to Montana with the local Trout Unlimited group for some serious angling on the fabled waters of the Madison River. But the Shad River right back here in Pennsylvania remained his favorite.

Jack didn't claim to be a poet but there was something about the Shad he couldn't quite put his finger on. He knew damn well that to the non-fishing crowd there was probably nothing special about the Shad. It was hardly the sort of stream that drew the canoeists, the kayakers searching for a white-water thrill. A narrow meandering sort of stream, its waters often ran shallow. In a dry summer, it became little more than a trickle in a lot of places, creating marginal trout water and lean economic times for him and Soothsayer. Summer brought a few hikers and campers but few anglers.

Before the arrival of the Great Green Drake Hatch the Shad had been a decently productive trout stream holding the usual amount and variety of insect hatches. It had a fly-fishing only section and a handful of the more noted members of the fly-fishing fraternity were known to occasionally make appearances at the stream. Then came the Green Drake Hatch. It had been something not unlike a religious awakening for the Shad.

When word got around about the first of the Green Drakes coming off the Shad in hordes at the end of May and early June that year it was never the same. The following spring, just as the Memorial Day

Weekend kicked off, cars, pickup trucks, RVs bearing license plates from states all up and down the East Coast and beyond packed the dirt parking lot around The Roll Cast and along Route 6 which ran parallel to the Shad. And every year thereafter the Green Drake Hatch seemed to draw more and more fly fishermen.

The stream's tranquility had been broken. No longer could a fisherman arrive at the Shad and pretty much depend on picking any spot along the stream and have it to himself. Prior to that, the stream had gained a grudging if growing acceptance from some of the fly-fishing fraternity after recovering from the ill effects of mine acid drainage.

In the 1930s, wells for the mine had been drilled along the banks of one of the Shad's feeder streams and though the mine had only operated for a few years, the enterprise was enough to ruin trout fishing until well after World War II. To hear Soothsayer tell it, the mining had eliminated the hordes of Green Drake insects known to gather along the Shad every spring.

Naturally, it was Soothsayer who discovered the hatch that late May evening years later, an event he had predicted for years.

Chapter 2

Soothsayer hadn't come by his nickname by accident. He had a way of foretelling truly strange or wonderful things that no one else dreamed of thinking up, the return of the Green Drake being just one such prediction. Once, he had prognosticated that Jack would win it big in the lottery. This was right around the time Jack was struggling to make ends meet, just after he'd been married, and the Shad was having one of its worst seasons, thanks to a summer of blistering hot weather that all but destroyed the trout fishing. By the end of July, many of the trout were found belly-up in the stream. It had been Jack's second season working as a guide and because of the trout kills, the fly fishermen weren't calling on his services.

The funny thing about that prediction was that Jack had never even played the lottery. And there was no way in hell Soothsayer could have known Jack had purchased a ticket that day in Williamsburg. Jack wasn't one to believe in luck. He was a strong believer in, as he put it, "making your own breaks in life." But then he'd won. It wasn't the big pot, but the eight thousand dollars was enough to keep the bill collectors away from him and Myra for a while.

Soothsayer had been right about other things too. There was Jack's marriage to Myra for one. Myra had always been on Jack about money. And eventually, it was furious squabbles over money which had ended the marriage. At least, money had seemed to be the cause of their marital woes. Back in those days, when his guide service business was just getting started, he'd spent more time fishing by himself than taking clients to the Shad.

He'd come into the store from the Shad after a long day, having pulled out of the stream dozens of hefty-sized trout on some fly he'd designed. There would be Soothsayer, his pipe in his mouth, sitting at his fly-tying vice, at work once again on one of his own insect imitations. Jack would be feeling pretty good about himself. He'd give Soothsayer the blow-by-blow account of the lunker trout he hooked from behind some boulder, about the perfect roll cast he'd made to land the fish. The new insect pattern would inevitably be introduced to the tourists coming up to the Shad for fishing. It was all part of business, making a living.

"Heh. Heh. Think about it. My name on a fly that Seth McNamee wouldn't be afraid to use."

Soothsayer nodded. He pulled on his pipe and looked past Jack toward the river.

"Nice guy Seth. Used to come here now and then and fish."

"I didn't know that."

"That was before he went … what do you call it? National?"

Soothsayer shook his head. "Ah yes. Fame, fortune. Can get in the way of a lot of things in life."

Soothsayer removed the pipe from his mouth and stared at it for a few moments, as if it held the very secret of life. He looked up at Jack. "How's the marriage these days?"

It was Soothsayer's way, his way of letting Jack know that there were priorities in life. Even now, Jack had to admit that Soothsayer had a way of getting at matters. The truth was, he had been spending too much time on the water to the exclusion of everything else—his guide business, his marriage. But then, it hadn't really mattered in the end. When the marriage finally came to its conclusion, Soothsayer's only words to Jack were, "Some men are meant to go at it alone."

"You mean life?" Jack asked.

"Something like that," Soothsayer said.

But all that had been years ago, well before the Green Drake Hatch and the onslaught of the tourists and the end of life as he had known it.

In those weeks of that year right before the return of the Green Drake Hatch, when things were still mostly slow around Green Spring Valley, Soothsayer had been busy. Night after night he sat in the back room of the Roll Cast, furiously tying Green Drake flies. Occasionally, other fly fishermen, wandering by to the nearby men's room after a few drinks at the bar, would spot Soothsayer hunched over the fly vice.

"What's old Soothsayer tying back there now?" they asked Jack, unable to decide for themselves if indeed the old man was crazy.

"Green Drakes."

"Green Drakes? Hell, that bug disappeared from here years ago."

Soothsayer was a laconic man, with a long beard, gnarled facial features and single lazy eye that tended to grow wide when he focused it on whomever he was speaking. To a stranger he might well have appeared like a wild, rustic hermit. Even those better acquainted with Soothsayer thought he was a little off his nut. More than one curious fisherman had asked him if he was tying Green Drakes to stock up for a trip downstate to Penns Creek, well known as having one of the most spectacular Green Drake hatches. Soothsayer only smiled and shook his head.

Soothsayer was a fine fly tier but most of the flies sold out of the Roll Cast were Jack's, but only because he tied a lot of the more popular patterns—the hendricksons, blue quills, blue-winged olive duns. Soothsayer tied a few of the them too, but he also liked to come up with his own creations—crazy combinations of fur and feathers and thread that no one had ever before seen.

Some of the flies he tied had caught them both good-sized trout over the years. Soothsayer did his fly tying, at least as far as Jack could tell, to get at something. It was as if creating flies that successfully caught fish served as a window into the very mystery of life. For Jack, fly-tying was more of a practical concern. Along with the guiding he did along the Shad and some of the local streams, the flies he tied and sold kept him fed, paid the bills and allowed him to buy his prized bamboo rods. "I don't live high on the hog," Jack liked to say. "But I do like my bamboo rods."

It had long been a source of humorous but authentic generational rivalry between the two men. Soothsayer had been using the same rod for the past forty years, an eight-foot bamboo he'd built that had been broken and repaired a half-dozen times over the four decades. Soothsayer affectionately called his rod, "Black Betsy," after the baseball bat used by former legendary ballplayer "Shoeless Joe" Jackson.

"Figures you'd use a rod named after a guy tossed out of baseball for throwing games," Jack said.

"They never proved that," Soothsayer said, gently stroking the rod. "Fact is, this rod is a wand that works like magic."

"Your ass," Jack said.

As much as they were different, as much as they argued back and forth about the whole business of catching trout, as wide a gap as existed in their ages and their attitudes toward life, Jack had to admit there were few people he could tolerate for any length of time longer than Soothsayer. There were men closer to his age with whom he could sit down and drink beer and discuss politics, the rotten state of the nation, and even the fine bodily contours of one of the local girls swilling a drink at the end of the bar.

There was Tar, for one. He was a big strapping fellow with a twinkle in his eye and a lusty laugh that shook the walls of the barroom. Tar had worked as a lumberjack until the local mill shut down and now tended bar for Soothsayer. Tar and Jack had gotten into any number of scrapes together when they'd been younger. But now Tar was married and faced with the heavy burden of putting food on the table for his wife and four kids.

The fact is there were few reasonably young men around Green Spring Valley anymore, what with the lumbering business having gone belly-up. In many ways that suited Jack just fine. He liked his solitude. He had long relished heading out on the Shad most nights to find a fishing hole all to himself. But there was the loneliness that gnawed at him, especially on long winter nights. Those evenings when he'd be at his fly-tying vice and the wind whistled through the pines and rattled the windows of his cabin. Many winter nights, when the cabin fever was just too much, he'd be down at the Roll Cast at the bar with the other locals, shooting the breeze with Tar while Soothsayer sat in the back tying his flies and getting ready to settle in for the evening.

Many of those nights would find him chasing home Tar and the few patrons who bothered venturing through the snow-covered narrow country roads to the Roll Cast. Soothsayer usually allowed Jack to close the place. There was often little to do. Run a wet rag down the bar, mop up the spilled beer from the floor, hand wash some of the dirty glasses and then lock up. Time was, when Jack would find himself near closing time sidling up to one of the young women left in the bar. Many of them had been only too eager for company and it hadn't been uncommon for Jack to spend the night with them back at his cabin or at their places.

Once, Jack had found himself on the wrong end of a gun held by a jealous husband. Rare was the man living in the Green Spring Valley who didn't own a gun and few of them needed much of an excuse to turn it on something other than wild game. But as Jack got older and perhaps wiser, the urge of chasing all those women began to wane. "Leads to a lot of problems Jack," Soothsayer said. And Jack realized it was true, that he was getting older and things were changing.

And then things had *really* changed with the Green Drake Hatch. Looking back, Jack couldn't say it was a situation that took him completely by surprise either. Soothsayer had, after all, predicted its return.

Soothsayer rarely traveled out of the Green Spring Valley. He didn't drive, didn't even own a car or have a drivers' license for that matter. And so, when Jack noticed Soothsayer tying all those Green Drakes during that long stretch from late winter into May, he'd been sure that the old fart was building up his stockpile for fishermen gearing up for trips to Penns Creek, or, that perhaps he'd gone off his nut.

And then, on that one evening in late May, Soothsayer came into the bar from the back room. Jack and Tar were at a table just finishing up supper—burgers and fries prepared by Tar's wife, Fay—when they saw him standing there, cradling in one arm his patched-up hip waders, his precious bamboo fly rod in his other hand, and a strange look on his face. Soothsayer slowly walked over to their table and announced in that soft whispery voice of his, "It's time."

"What the hell are you talkin' about?" Tar asked.

"The Green Drake," Soothsayer said, tilting his head back and tightly squeezing his eyes shut as if not doing so would allow something precious to escape him. "It's time."

Without another word, he sat down in an empty chair at their table to begin pulling on his hip waders.

"Hell," Tar said. "I'll get a car of worms from the back and follow you down."

Jack fought a smile and shook his head. Tar well knew of the deep reverence Soothsayer had for fly-fishing and liked nothing better than to poke some fun at it. Nothing pissed off a true fly fisherman more than sharing a stretch of stream with some "bait caster." Jack couldn't make light of it though. After all, his buddy had been right about these things before. Still, Jack wondered if possibly Soothsayer's deep well of psychic powers had run dry.

Chapter 3

Jack was just about convinced Soothsayer had perhaps gone batty as he found himself being led by Soothsayer to The Bend, a shallow, unproductive and altogether unremarkable stretch of the Shad about one hundred yards down from the old Boy Scout camp. In recent weeks, Soothsayer, never a garrulous or gregarious sort anyway, had become even more quiet, remaining pretty much holed up in his room above the Roll Cast.

Soothsayer was just past his seventy-fifth birthday, and there seemed to be indications that possibly the slow, but relentless steps of death were creeping closer. Only in the most recent days had Soothsayer displayed his old self. The gleam had returned to his one good eye, and on the way down to the stream, there was a bounce in his stride.

When they arrived around dusk, not a fish was rising, at least, none that Jack could see. Nor did he expect anything in the way of a feeding frenzy of trout.

Once upon a time, The Bend had been a marvelous trout hole. Men now long dead had talked of Brown Trout thirty inches long grabbing Green Drakes from off the surface.

"I tied on a number eight Green Drake back at The Roll Cast son," Soothsayer said.

"Sure. Okay," Jack said.

Jack would have resented being called son by anyone other than Soothsayer, but from the old man it just felt right. If Jack thought about it, there weren't a whole lot of people in this world he really respected. The politicians, the televangelists, the businessmen with the fat wallets–he surely didn't hold much respect for them. With Soothsayer, he had always felt a bond, and so, he was just fine with Soothsayer calling him son. But this was one time it suddenly felt strange.

Around Soothsayer he often felt like a younger hand in the presence of wise guru–even if it was him who was supposed to be the local fishing legend. Now, watching Soothsayer studying the stream, he thought the old man looked like an old fool. It had grown increasingly darker by the stream, and as far as Jack could tell, there wasn't going to be any kind of hatch coming off.

"What do you say we head back?" Jack said. "We don't want to be walking back to the Roll Cast in the dark." He didn't like the thought of his old friend stumbling through the darkness in his waders. He didn't want to have to take him by the arm to ensure he didn't fall on his face.

But Soothsayer just stood there gazing at the water. In another moment, he began slowly wading into foot-deep water as he kept his eye across the stream where the water curled around a fallen log.

Jack looked at his watch. It was now quarter to nine, and still no fish were rising. The sight of Soothsayer standing nearly knee deep in the still waters of the Shad seemed a bit pathetic, even sad. Jack suddenly recalled what Soothsayer had told him on more than one occasion, how when his "time came" he wanted to die right out on the stream with his fly rod in his hand. "And if I'm lucky I'll be bringing up a fat Brown Trout," he added.

Jack liked the image. In fact, he too thought that catching a big trout would make for a pretty good send-off into the next world. One thing was for sure: they both shared a love of trout streams and hefty Brown Trout. Death wasn't something Jack liked to consider for too long a time. It was one of those gray areas in life that a man apparently had no control over. And if there was one thing Jack liked it was being in control, being the captain of his ship. He had he built his whole life around that very concept.

At twenty-five, he'd given up a decent paying union job at the mill in Williamsburg to come up here and do things his way. Tying flies and hiring himself out as a fishing guide sure as hell wasn't big money, but it kept him out from under the thumb of some boss, in the outdoors and near the stream he loved. And isn't that what he had always wanted? Soothsayer, who in those days was nothing to Jack but an occasional fishing partner, had rented him out a room in the back for his fly-tying and a one-bedroom apartment upstairs for him and Myra, his new bride. It was the set-up he'd been looking for since the fly-fishing bug had bitten him. And as far as he was concerned, it had worked out well enough.

Not that there weren't problems. Myra had forever been on him in those days about opening a fly shop down in the city after he began building up somewhat of a local reputation for himself as a fisherman and guide, but he knew the moment he started driving to work and dealing with rods and equipment and all the inventory and the hassles of running a store in some strip mall, he'd be putting one foot in the grave. And then Myra had become more of a pain in the ass about it all. Money, she said, needed to be socked away. The future had to be considered. It was just as well that the marriage had ended as far as Jack was concerned.

There was just enough light left in the sky to perhaps see a fly hit the water when Soothsayer announced that the hatch had started. And with that, he made a few false casts before letting his line disappear into the fading light and fall somewhere out in front of him on the water.

Jack saw nothing. A Green Drake hatch, at least the kind he'd seen on Penns Creek and other streams known to give birth to that mayfly, often came off with a flurry of life above the water. When the Green Drakes, newly hatched from the stream, failed to take flight from the water they became easy meals for trout. On some streams, particularly Penns Creek, the air became so thick with the drakes that fishermen were known to swallow mouthfuls of them.

And then, it happened.

A brief burst of wind stirred the air. In the next moment, a flurry of bugs appeared. Jack felt a few of the insects hit his face.

"It's on Jack," Soothsayer called out with a joyous yelp from the stream's dark waters.

Darkness enveloped the stream, but Jack clearly saw rings forming on the surface. Dozens of trout were making splashy rises for the bugs.

Soothsayer brought back his rod right after the splash, leaving no doubt that a fish of some size was on the line. Soothsayer was in command right away—as Jack knew he would be.

Though Soothsayer in his advanced years avoided the deeper holes and rarely ventured near any potentially treacherous fast-moving water, he had few peers when it came to actually catching fish. He gave the trout some line, played him briefly and brought the fish under control. Stooping to the water and carefully scooping him into his net, he informed Jack that the Brown Trout he'd hooked was sixteen inches.

Soothsayer no sooner freed the fish when he hooked another one. It looked to Jack to be about nine inches. With just two casts Soothsayer had caught a pair of fish.

"You might want to give it a try Jack," Soothsayer said. "This is something."

For a moment Jack considered heading back to his cabin for his rod. It was only about a ten-minute walk. Who knew? Perhaps the hatch would continue. But then he figured … no. This was Soothsayer's time.

Jack saw the rings still forming on the water as Soothsayer released the trout and inspected his leader and fly. The bugs were thick in the air, unlike any hatch he had ever seen—anywhere.

In front of Soothsayer, fish rose everywhere for bugs, some of them leaping from the stream to grab flies. Soothsayer, though, had decided to target in on a single fish. On the far side of the stream, away from where many of the trout were rising, the large dark head of a trout Jack estimated to be close to ten pounds was occasionally breaking the surface to grab Green Drakes. In fact, in the dying light of this spring evening, Jack wasn't sure it was a trout, but perhaps one of the stream's otters known to populate The Shad.

Soothsayer took a few steps farther into the water toward the spot. But he was still a good seventy-five feet away. Distance wasn't the big problem, however. Somehow, Soothsayer would have to get the fly out in front of the monster trout by allowing it to sweep in a smooth flow toward the fish. No easy task. The current was fast there and didn't push the water in a straight flow. Instead, the water flowed against a boulder before dividing and spilling into a short pool where the trout was feeding under a willow tree. The tree, with its long branches spreading out onto the water like spray from a fountain, was an easy target for an angler's fly. To catch the mammoth trout would require a cast of precise accuracy.

Jack wasn't a betting man. The odds were never good enough for him to risk what money he had on games of chance. But as he watched Soothsayer slowly take up his rod and begin throwing out line and twirling it in a loop above him, he figured this was one bet he'd make that his old buddy wouldn't catch this fish.

Jack never saw the fly hit the water. A few early season lightning bugs, appearing like the last smoldering coals of a campfire, flickered among the thick brush on the far bank. He could, however, see Soothsayer mending out line to keep the fly on a true course toward the fish. This would be the tricky part. Too much tension on the line and the fly would be grabbed by the current and not go anywhere near the fish, but too much slack or bow in the line would either send the trout scurrying for cover or alert it to simply ignore the offering.

Jack thought he saw Soothsayer's Green Drake fly shoot from out of the fast flow just behind the boulder. The water's surface thundered with a splash. Soothsayer's line tightened, and for a moment the old fisherman lost his footing before bracing himself. He raised the rod tip, and in the next moment, the rod bent like a horseshoe. Furiously, he began feeding out line to the trout. The fish wasn't going to make it easy at all.

Jack rushed down to the stream bank for a closer look. In his long life, Soothsayer had caught his share of large fish, but Jack wondered if his angling skills were still up to landing this one. It was obvious to Jack that this fish was a true Shad River lunker. He hoped like hell Soothsayer could pull it off. The two of them had shared many great times together out on the stream, and when one of them was into a trophy trout, it was always special.

A struggle ensued, a kind of cat-and-mouse game between a fisherman and his prey. Soothsayer let the fish take off in a mad rush to one end of the pool before furiously reeling in line, only to have the trout take off on another wild sprint. Jack well knew that surge of energy that ran up the rod and into your hands and arms, your entire body, when a fish, with the fly embedded in its mouth, tore to the depths of the pool and suddenly leaped from the water, unleashing a spray as it tried desperately to throw the hook. There was nothing quite like it. Soothsayer was engaged in such a fight.

Soothsayer remained calm. In his many years of guiding Jack had seen far too many less experienced anglers lose a large fish on that first run. In their eagerness to land that trout they long fantasized having stuffed and mounted over the fireplace of their suburban dens, they desperately reeled in line. These were often young men, vigorous and healthy, their movements quick, their reflexes sharp, but lacking the fishing skills and experience for landing elusive and wily trout. Soothsayer was a seasoned, savvy angler, but far from a young man. And Jack wondered if perhaps Soothsayer's time had passed, that his angling skills were but a distant memory. He spent virtually no time fishing any longer, instead spending his time holed up in the store tying his flies, dreaming his dreams and growing older.

It got quiet. Soothsayer held the rod with both hands tightly gripping it above his head, but he was otherwise a still figure there in the water. Had he lost this great fish? Or had the fish merely tired? And then the water's surface churned. The dark image of Soothsayer seemed to stumble as he made his way a few steps farther into the water. He stopped and pulled back his rod. His reel screamed, and Jack knew, Soothsayer was into his backing, with the fish making perhaps one final mad run to escape.

Soothsayer moved unsteadily farther and deeper into the stream with the rod tip up. For most of this struggle Soothsayer had been in water no higher than his knees. But now the water was up to his waist and the old man, apparent now to Jack only as a shadow in the darkness, was creeping still farther out. Jack felt it was time to stop his fishing buddy. Catching a hog trout was one thing, but risking your life was quite another.

He remembered some of his own struggles over the years with trout. Once, during a cold December day he'd hooked onto a steelhead making a run out of Lake Erie, chasing it a good two hundred yards down a tributary swollen with snow melt. That hadn't been the brightest thing he'd ever done in his life. Hell, he had nearly drowned. But he'd caught the damn fish all right– a thirty-inch steelhead he'd had stuffed for display back at the Roll Cast. Jack had known Soothsayer to go the distance with a fish or two as well. But a lot of years had passed since those days.

And then, the struggle apparently ended. By now, it was quite dark at The Bend. The old fisherman appeared only as a shadowy silhouette against the trees. With the rod tip up, he slowly reeled in line. The question was whether Soothsayer won or lost this epic battle with this great fish. Jack held his breath as the old man retreated a few steps and began reeling in line. Jack could hear his heavy breathing, see his labored movements.

"You okay Sooth?"

Soothsayer said nothing. He felt sure that the old man had lost the fish, but the old man fooled him.

"I've always said Jack that if you go fishing for the lunkers, always bring a net."

Chapter 4

Soothsayer continued tying flies there in the back of the store, but Jack, for one, could see he wasn't quite the same. There was a general weariness about him now, a halting manner in his gait. He limped more than ever, dragging his bad leg behind him.

Somehow, as such things often happen, word got out about the return of the Green Drake to The Shad. A Green Drake hatch normally lasts about two weeks before it flickers out, like candles from a breeze, before returning the same time the following year. And it was in that next year that fly fishermen began showing up in droves to fish the hatch.

Its arrival the next year, just as the Memorial Day Weekend was kicking off, sent the clear message that things were never to be the same. Jack counted more than three dozen vehicles parked along the roadside area near Paddy's Hole one night during the hatch. A popular fishing spot thanks to its easy access and holding area for big trout, Paddy's Hole was a good mile from The Bend.

And so, the Shad returned to its former glory. Jack was soon guiding more people around The Shad and to its feeder streams known to hold wild Brook Trout. The campground up the road from the Roll Cast near Logan's Bluff became increasingly crowded. Campers, jeeps and four-wheel drive vehicles, many of them with out-of-state license plates, roared past the Roll Cast and along the two-lane road.

Jack found himself tending more and more to business. For years, anyone needing a guide had merely to call the Roll Cast and ask for one, which of course meant Jack. Soothsayer always knew his old fishing buddy was only a phone call away. Now, with the flurry of fishermen waiting to try out The Shad, it was all Jack could do to keep up with the requests. Eventually, he had installed in his cabin a hot line where people could reach him.

Times were good. For the first time in his life Jack was putting away some money. He bought some expensive bamboo rods, had a room built onto his cabin which he used exclusively for an office and as a place for his fly-tying. He began leaving hefty tips on the bar for Tar. Tar, in turn, began referring to him as "Diamond Jack." Jack thought it was great. He was far from anything even approaching wealthy, but his financial situation had surely improved. No longer did he have to put off leaky roof problems or other house repair jobs.

He basically maintained his same lifestyle, taking his meals at the Roll Cast and spending the bulk of his free time either tying flies or drinking beer. That is, what free time he had. Most days during fishing season he came back to his cabin exhausted from another day of guiding. But the physical demands were only part of it. Many of the people he guided he found exasperating.

In the past, a good week of work amounted to two or three days of guiding, much of which consisted of nothing more than five or six hours on the water with some single fisherman or groups of anglers who just wanted to know where they could either catch a lot of trout or latch onto a lunker or two. Quite often, they were competent enough anglers, but completely unfamiliar with The Shad and merely needed some help finding their way around the stream. Now, not only was he guiding six and seven days a week, he was taking people out to the water who "didn't know the end of a fly rod from their Aunt Sally's left toe," as Soothsayer put it. They were a new breed. Tar called them, "Yuppie assholes."

Jack watched them pull up to the Roll Cast in their foreign cars and outfitted in expensive neoprene waders and bamboo rods for which they'd plunked down thousands of dollars. And so many of them were demanding. They expected the water to run gin clear, for the fish to bite on every fly they cast. When it didn't work out quite that way, there could be hell to pay. Too many of these snooty folks, Jack concluded, were too accustomed to having their way, hot shot businessmen and physicians and money managers who pushed underlings about and made everyone else's lives miserable.

There was the guy who'd talked of fishing the big streams with the huge trout out in Montana—a real pain in the ass. He had arrived at The Shad expecting to be treated like royalty. The fact that he hadn't found the sort of lodging "as I found in West Yellowstone" was a tip-off to Jack that he'd be dealing with a prima donna. Once out on the water he'd handed Jack his rod and waited for him to tie on a fly. Jack handed the rod right back to him. "Not my job fella," he said.

It was just the beginning of a horrible day. The man expected nothing less than to hook up with monster trout. He'd even worn a glove on his casting hand and told Jack with a straight face that he was a dry fly purist. The fact that he'd arrived at the Shad during a time of day and when the conditions weren't conducive to rising trout didn't deter him. He fully anticipated finding dozens of trout splashing and leaping about the stream "just like on the Madison River." When no trout rose, he made it known that he didn't think much of The Shad or Jack's guiding for that matter.

More than once, Jack had suggested to the gentleman that he might well try fishing nymphs or wet flies. The guy pushed on in a futile dry-flying mission as if to prove Jack wrong. "I don't need to cheat to catch trout," he said.

It was well past lunch, and a steady drizzle fell, when the man finally did, remarkably enough, land his single fish of the day on a dry fly–a nice seventeen-inch Brown Trout that he would have lost if Jack hadn't been there with the net to scoop it out of the water. Things got sticky then. The man insisted on having the fish mounted. He'd seen a sign for a taxidermist on his way to the Shad earlier that day and wanted to go their immediately. Jack reminded him they were fishing in a catch-and-release section.

"It goes back to the stream," Jack said.

"One fish. Who will know?" the man said.

Jack said he'd know, and that's all that mattered.

It was after the guy said he was damn well going to keep the fish, and no "second rate guide" could tell him he couldn't, that Jack put a firm grip on the guy's arm. That did if for the man. He took the sort of wild roundhouse swing that couldn't have caught a blind man in a drunken stupor by surprise. Jack stepped back and caught the man flush on the nose with an uppercut.

The police came the next day after the man had filed charges, and Jack might have spent some time in the county lockup had not Soothsayer intervened. Charges were quickly dropped provided Jack didn't accept the guiding fee.

After that unfortunate episode, Jack found himself putting on his best smile for the clients.

Soothsayer had helped Jack escape scrapes in the past, and he was never above offering words of wisdom to his old buddy or even scolding him if necessary. He knew damn well that he was the only person who could get away with it. He realized Jack was beyond stubborn, occasionally hot-tempered and not above resorting to fisticuffs to settle a dispute. And he had a good handle as to why he behaved that way.

Soothsayer had known Jack's old man, "as nasty of a son-of-a bitch if ever there was one." A man who had taken out much of that ill temper on Jack and his mother. A lumberjack with a reckless thirst for drink and women, he eventually came to a violent end in a barroom dispute.

As Soothsayer liked to say to Jack, "as mean a coot as your old man was, there's always someone nastier."

They were words Jack had taken to heart. There had been times when he had found himself in some real touchy situations in barrooms. Maybe he'd been lingering a bit too long at the legs of a woman sitting with her burly redneck boyfriend. Or, under the influence of too many beers, he'd spoken out of turn to the construction crew unwinding in the bar. Jack realized there were times a little bullshit, a joke, a little laughter to keep things calm, were the best course of action.

In his more reflective moments, which seemed to be more frequent as he grew older, Jack could see the utter folly of it all. Why be like his father, who'd been known to stomp the hell out of men who crossed him? Inevitably, someone could pull out a gun, or unleash a knife and stab you to death, as had happened to his old man.

"Big Jim" McAllister had been a strapping ox of a man, who'd used his girth to great advantage when the poorly organized lumber union needed a chief goon to crack some heads during labor disputes that arose. The fact that he was in many ways a lot like Big Jim was never lost on Jack. Violence had been big a part of his upbringing, an accepted and often effective means of gaining the upper hand. Explanations, diplomacy, verbal communication of any sort held little sway with Big Jim once he had his mind made up to beat the crap out of Jack or his now long-dead mother.

And so, Jack had believed early on that talking achieved little in the way of settling wars. Words had been of little use in the McAllister household. And yet, as he grew older and slower to anger, he came to realize it was impossible to win every fight, and to go through life like Big Jim McAllister—raging at the world, eager to end any dispute with a good ass-kicking. Hell, resorting to violence was almost like surrendering to the old man. Why dredge up the ghost of his father? When he'd taken a poke at that snooty Yuppie it had been more than a few years since he'd been in any sort of fight.

Even well into his thirties Jack had kept trim, but not through any rigorous or structured exercise program. He'd never thought much of the types who stayed in shape by hitting the gyms, jogging, or as he put it:

"running their asses off for no reason at all." Jack had stayed in reasonable shape by performing everyday tasks—chopping wood for his fireplace, doing carpentry work or lending a hand to barroom buddies with heavy labor around their homes. Someone always needed a hand hefting junk or heavy furniture onto a truck, digging a septic tank, shingling a house, or God knows what else.

No one who lived around the Green Valley had much money, and everyone seemed to help each other out with construction and digging and roofing and even bailing water out of basements when The Shad River overflowed. And then, there was all the walking he'd done through the hills and woods of the Green Valley. But now, he seemed to have less time for those activities. His business was growing with his waistline. He laughed when Tar, whose own belly seemed to expand with each passing year, kidded him about drinking too much beer.

Truth be told, Jack wasn't putting away the beer as he once had. There'd been a time when he'd done a lot of drinking. Back in the day, it had been a rare night when he wasn't at a bar stool in the Roll Cast hoisting a few with the boys. It was all he could do anymore to find time to go into the bar. Each night he came home dog tired from another full day of guiding clients. It was a mad furious rush many evenings to get in his fly tying. Some nights, he fell asleep face-down across his fly-tying table. And then it was always up the next morning to guide another client.

Soothsayer suggested he find a part-timer to help him out with the guiding. Tar was a help sometimes, but he usually had more work than he could handle at the Roll Cast. Finding another part-timer would mean the kind of headaches Jack didn't feel like dealing with. Always used to working alone, he wanted to keep it that way.

"I gave up that factory job fifteen years ago with the intention of being my own boss and boss nobody else," he told Soothsayer. "And I'm sure as shit going to keep things that way."

Each day, starting in that year following the return of the Green Drake hatch, Soothsayer would watch Jack trudge into the Roll Cast and collapse into a chair at his usual table to eat his lunch or dinner. What had happened to his old buddy? That guy who'd always rolled into the bar with the strutting, confident strides of the high school football running back he'd once been, to exchange put-downs and one-liners with Tar.

"What are those damn things?" Tar asked.

Jack rolled the small plastic cylindrical pill container about in his one hand.

"Ginseng," Jack whispered as he looked around in case someone had wandered into the otherwise empty barroom on this rainy evening. "Suppose to make you feel energetic and vigorous."

"Heh Heh. I got your vigorous right here," Tar said, pointing with a stubby finger at his groin.

"It comes from the root of the Ginseng tree," Soothsayer said. He sat next to Jack at a stool looking with much interest at the pills enclosed in the small brown container. "Used to be a fella lived up on the ridge who grew that stuff along with a bunch of other herbs he bottled and sold. Strange old guy. Lived to be a hundred and one."

A Johnny Cash song was playing softly on the juke box behind them. Much to the consternation of Tar and Jack, who both loathed what they called "shit kicker music", Soothsayer had kept the machine well stocked with country music tunes.

"They got pills for everything nowadays," Tar laughed. "Little green ones to help you get it up, even little red ones to bring it down."

Jack winced. It was just the kind of stuff he didn't want to hear. He never dreamed he'd be taking vitamins. He'd long felt that vitamins for a pick-me-up or God knows what else were for the New Age crowd. But the long days guiding had been taking their toll and well …

"They doin' anything for ya?" Tar asked.

Jack shrugged. He didn't know if the pills had done a damn thing for him. He only started taking them a week earlier at the advice of one of his clients, one of the well-educated, lean, tanned elites who seemed to be taking up fly fishing any more. The guy had seemed like a pleasant enough sort though, and not a bad fisherman either. Somehow the two of them had gotten to talking about healthy lifestyles and that sort of crap, and Jack had let it drop about how he hadn't been feeling all that energetic of late. In addition to taking ginseng, the guy had suggested Jack cut out red meat from his diet and take up yoga. Jack had laughed and agreed to at least give the ginseng a try.

"Might be something to them pills," Soothsayer said. "Then again …"

"Ha. Just lay off the sauce for a while," Tar said, reaching across the bar to give Jack a lusty pat on the back. "Better yet, pour yourself a good stiff one before you go to bed every night."

"I've been laying off the booze a bit," Jack said. "Guess I'm not as young as I used to be."

"Hell. Who is," Tar said. "The other night my old lady wanted to do it the way we used to when we was first married."

Jack grinned. Tar was forever sharing bits of his sex life to anyone who would listen. Funny thing was, even after all these years, he never grew tired of listening to it, even if it was hard to filter out the bullshit from the truth. The image of Tar and his wife doing the dirty deed? It was something he would just as soon not think about. Both were big and shaped like ripe old watermelons, and it was difficult to imagine the two of them in the heat of passion doing much besides roll about atop the huge waterbed they had placed in the bedroom of their mountain shack. Tar's embellishments aside, he didn't doubt that Tar and Fay enjoyed a somewhat satisfying sex life. Even after more than twenty years of marriage and four kids they carried on like newlyweds, giggling, grabbing at each's butts and sometimes even chasing each other around the barroom, scenes that often played out to the amusement of the bar's patrons, but annoyed, even embarrassed Soothsayer.

Soothsayer offered up the excuse that such shenanigans weren't good for his business, but judging from the grins on the mugs of the salty old men in the barroom, that surely was not the case. Besides, Jack knew as much as anyone that Soothsayer was not that greatly concerned about making plenty of money off The Roll Cast. The same patrons had been frequenting the place for years anyway for the cheap draught beer, and they weren't about to drive miles away to find the next closest barroom. And business had even picked up with the return of the Green Drake Hatch.

Any reference to sex bothered Soothsayer. Often, he left the barroom when Tar either told a dirty joke or managed to shift the barroom discussion to sex. Other times, Soothsayer sat and endured Tar's lusty tales, but not without nervously twitching in his seat.

"Yeah. Ol' Fay wanted me to do the fireman's carry," Tar continued.

Jack raised a hand. "Never mind. We don't need to hear anymore."

"Aw c'mon. I was just gettin' to the good part."
At this, Tar winked lasciviously at Soothsayer who sat
at the bar with his head down, looking as if he just
wanted the floor to swallow him up.

"Let's just say Fay and me ain't as young as we
used to be," Tar added.

Jack turned his attention back to the bottle of pills
before him on the bar. The talk of growing old was
depressing. "Well, I ain't as young as I used to be either.
That's for damn sure."

Tar grunted and lit up a cigarette. The barroom
grew silent, save for the Johnny Cash number
continuing to play softly on the jukebox. Soothsayer
stirred in his seat. Then, in a few moments, he began to
cough, softly at first, before the coughs grew louder,
deeper in his chest. In another moment, he let loose with
a torrent of uncontrollable hacking.

Tar squirted some water into a glass from the sink
behind the bar and placed it before Soothsayer. Out of
the corner of his eye Jack watched his old buddy, like a
sun-scorched desert traveler parched from the heat,
eagerly take up the glass and with a trembling hand, lift
it to his quivering lips and gulp down the water. That
done, Soothsayer managed to place the glass rather
unsteadily down on the bar.

"You okay?" Jack asked.

Soothsayer didn't seem to hear the question. He
had one of his gnarled old hands on the bar to steady

himself. His attention seemed to be on the barroom's saw-dusted floor. Jack had known his buddy long enough to know something heavy weighed on his mind, something he was dying to share. Soothsayer raised his hand and focused his one good eye right on Jack.

"Go down by the stream," he said. "Go down by the stream and sit under a tree. Listen to the birds call to each other. Watch the squirrels scurry for nuts. Look at the trees in their spring splendor. Watch the trout rise for bugs."

Jack felt Soothsayer's single eye boring right through him as if into his very soul. Such advice, coming from someone other than Soothsayer, would have sounded utterly silly. The old man's words were straight from the heart.

Chapter 5

Soothsayer wanted to help Jack. As a businessman himself, if not an altogether successful one, he knew what a growing enterprise could do to a man. It was clear to him that Jack, for the first time in his life, was getting a scent of money. And Soothsayer wasn't sure he liked it.

Soothsayer had long known of the controlling force money could have on a person. As a young man he'd put every dollar he had into starting up the Roll Cast, which at the time was no more than a long-abandoned old fishing cabin off Route 6, swallowed up by years of neglect and Mother Nature and assailed by vandals. It seemed beyond saving with its sagging front porch, leaky roof, broken windows, and vines of poison ivy, tall sumac and thickets of weeds shrouding its front. But Soothsayer had a vision. Slowly, he refurbished and resurrected the place, first selling fishing bait and the flies he tied and a few assorted items. Eventually, he rented out the few rooms upstairs.

It was a break-even venture, but if nothing else, it provided a roof over his head and served as his own little piece of paradise tucked away in the foothills. He didn't need or require much, and he found he was quite happy being his own boss. One thing was for sure: It beat the heck out of breaking his back as a laborer for the Pennsylvania Railroad. Even as a young man, Soothsayer had realized there was little future in toiling for someone else. Even through all the lean years, when it was all he could do to keep the place running, he knew things could be worse.

Soothsayer didn't figure he had the personal makeup of what could be called business acumen. He kept his operation small, his only concessions to growth amounting to having a couple of gas pumps put in and building a single addition onto the building for a tiny kitchen and a small barroom where patrons could grab a sandwich or a beer.

His little enterprise kept him busy, but not so busy that it became all-consuming. He did little advertising and loathed billboards, claiming they "fouled up God's landscape." More than one patron had told him he was foolish not to announce his business along Route 6.

For years, there had been virtually nothing in the way of eateries or rest stops for weary motorists traveling the many empty miles along that road between Williamsburg and the New York State line save for the Roll Cast, yet he held no desire to turn the place into something more.

It amused him to no end when they showed up at the Roll Cast, businessmen in suits driving expensive cars, the unmistakable scent of money about them, with offers to buy him out. Some were speculators, chasing the notion that Route 6 was someday to expand to four lanes, bringing more traffic to the area and with it, more travelers, more enterprises, more dollars.

Soothsayer found it all distasteful.

"One thing I don't need is to spend my free time tucked away in the room out back wondering in heaven's name what to do with a bunch of extra money," he said.

Soothsayer had been raised in a small cabin just over the mountain from the Roll Cast. In the time he'd worked for the railroad down in Williamsburg he'd missed everything about the hills: The crisp air with the scent of pines and things fresh and alive, the fog-shrouded spring and fall mornings, the sound of The Shad roaring through the valley. He loved being able to rise from his bed for morning strolls through the woods and to come upon the occasional campers and fishermen stirring from their slumbers, the aroma of a smoking camp fire and of fresh bacon sizzling.

He loved showing up at the Shad at dawn, to listen to the water thunder through the forest or dapple gently over the rocks into a pool. He especially liked to be at the Shad for the morning hatches, when the trout were rising to slurp insects from the surface. It wasn't important that he have a fly rod ready to pull from the water any number of the hungry stream-bred Brook or Brown Trout. Just being there was his reward.

From his fishing vest, he'd pull out a diary and mark down the precise times the different flies were hatching. He kept meticulous records of the stream's insect hatches, visiting the stream daily to watch the various bugs floating, dancing, dropping to the water, where waiting trout rose to swallow them. Anglers were kept informed of the day's hatches by the information he scribbled on the chalkboard nailed to the wall back at the Roll Cast in the little corner where he sold his flies and other fly-fishing items.

On warm nights, after a long day in the store tending to the anglers and the restaurant patrons and other customers, he liked to sit in his rocking chair on the Roll Cast's sprawling front porch with its creaky wooden floorboards, taking in the sound of a thrush calling to a mate or watching an autumn leaf fall to the ground. Other evenings, he headed off to the Shad for a couple of hours of fishing. This was the best part of the day of all.

No matter what pressing duties were back at the Roll Cast, he liked to set aside time for some evening fishing. Often, he fished with Jack, whose intensity and stream-side histrionics amused him. Jack simply *had* to catch fish. For Jack, there was no other reason for these evening visits to the Shad. A trout he failed to hook left him screaming, cursing the heavens, while Soothsayer delighted in the simplicity of caddis flies dancing over riffles.

Soothsayer was not an especially religious man, but he felt God had assigned him the drudgery of first working for the railroad to warn him he was meant to return home and live this much simpler, back-to-nature existence. Here, in the hills where the Shad River ran, he had found sanity and a degree of happiness in his life. Jack, his longtime buddy, shared his philosophy about the land, but he worried that his friend was losing sight of what was important.

Soothsayer considered Jack the closest thing he had to a son, and while he didn't spend every waking moment worrying about his happiness, he wanted greatly to help him. Too often, he figured his advice to him came off sounding too much like the fundamentalist mountain preachers he'd endured as a kid. He didn't want to jam anything down Jack's throat, but at the same time he hoped he'd heed his words. And now, he was watching him get caught up and distressed over money matters. He knew it often took something drastic–a brush with death perhaps–for a man to change his outlook on things. He wondered how long Jack could continue with the pace he kept.

What had the return of the Green Drake Hatch meant? Often, Soothsayer pondered this. It certainly had brought to the Shad an awful lot of fishermen who otherwise wouldn't have come, folks who were able to join in a memorable fishing experience. And Soothsayer had watched his own financial fortunes grow, thanks to the surge of patrons coming to the Roll Cast. Then again, this invasion of people had interrupted the quiet rustic setting, not to mention the fishing.

Each evening that spring, he had watched his old fishing buddy come in to the Roll Cast for yet another quick supper, his eyes heavy with the burden of another long day on the stream, looking for all the world like he needed more than anything to sleep for a good month. And now, this talk of vitamins. It just wasn't like Jack. He just needed, Soothsayer thought, to cut back a little on the guiding and do more fishing and relaxing.

And yet, it was becoming harder and harder for everyone to make ends meet. A lot of folks just had to work like dogs. That was the way it was anymore. No one wanted to hire anybody, and no employers wanted to pay much of anything, and the whole damn economy was suffering for it. Just in the last couple of years that fact had been driven home to him as sure as a deer running from buckshot. Prices kept rising. The food he bought for the restaurant, the fur and feathers he purchased to tie his flies—all of it was getting costlier.

Heck, if he was a young man now he doubted if he would be able to afford starting up a business. And while Jack, in his mind at least, was still a youngster, he could see some point to his buddy wanting to build up a bank account. Jack didn't seem to have time to spend his money on anything. Six and seven days a week he was out on the water guiding another client. And except for that addition he'd put on to his cabin and those expensive bamboo rods he'd bought, the money apparently was burning in Jack's pocket.

Soothsayer didn't believe in prying into another fellow's finances, but he wondered if Jack was planning on something big with his money. That often happened to a man. The money sits around for too long, and when something turns a man's head it can be gone just like that. Jack hadn't breathed a word about what he planned to with any extra cash, but Soothsayer had an uneasy feeling. He'd seen enough men with new-found wealth sink money into one thing or another without careful consideration. Heck, how many times had he received offers to go partners in some Godforsaken business start-up of some kind? And Jack, he well knew, could be reckless and impulsive. He just hoped to creation that

Jack wasn't linking up with Adamly. That would be a fatal mistake.

Chapter 6

Normally, Soothsayer tried to banish all thoughts of Adamly from his mind. As he'd grown longer in the tooth he'd found that bad thoughts often upset his stomach.

Adamly had just ambled into the bar in that cocksure way of his with a girl young enough to be his daughter hanging on his arm. Soothsayer wondered how he could make a sudden exit without directing too much attention to himself. The last thing he wanted was to be in the same barroom with the guy. It was the typical Adamly grand entrance, a man who never failed to sweep into the barroom without making sure everyone knew he had arrived. Soothsayer couldn't help but notice the girl, the usual Adamly model: a pretty, cheap-looking, dumbstruck thing who no doubt found it flattering to be with a big shot lawyer.

"Howdy folks," Adamly said with a huge smile. "Everyone. Meet Goldy."

Soothsayer didn't even bother excusing himself from the barroom. He wasn't feeling particularly great anyway. The coughing spell had left his chest aching and he knew hanging around to listen to Adamly would only make him feel worse.

Jack and Tar exchanged knowing smiles. Both had grown used to seeing Adamly show up in the barroom with these young girls. It had become a standing joke that as Adamly grew older, the girls he brought into the bar seemed to grow younger.

"Goldy huh," Tar said. "I once knew someone named Goldy. Nice girl. Best little dancer in a G-string I ever seen. The things she could do with a dollar bill would make your eyes spin."

Adamly winked his eye at Jack as he steered the giggling Goldy toward a bar stool. "Goldy here's going to be a secretary. She's studying hard down there in Williamsburg at the business school. Isn't that right honey?"

Goldy took the compliment as an excuse to nuzzle her nose into Adamly's shoulder, allowing him to lean in and give her a quick kiss.

"Hot damn," said Tar, slapping the bar top. "Ain't love grand?"

The sudden presence of Adamly in the barroom made Jack feel uneasy. Oh, he liked Adamly well enough. Hell, it was hard not to like the guy. The two of them had shared enough good times together. And if friendship can be based on the bonding of two men that included heavy drinking and chasing women, then Jack guessed the two of them were probably something like friends. But just lately, their relationship had changed a bit.

Adamly needed a favor from Jack, but unlike past ones, which usually involved sharing the phone number of the woman with the nice legs sitting at the far end of the bar, this one had financial considerations attached to it.

Adamly wanted Jack to go partners with him in buying some land about five miles up the river. Jack knew the area well. The Flats. It was a very remote area of the Green Spring Valley, virtually nothing there in the way of human habitation, the only sign of any civilization being the presence of an exclusive private hunting and fishing club about fifty yards from the Shad. It was easy to see why the club, known quite appropriately as The Flats Hunting and Fishing Club, had been plunked down in that spot.

Here, The Shad's normal meandering and gentle flow burst forth in spectacular white water. From a steep hillside, the stream thundered through a gorge of sheer rock, cascading between and around and over garage-sized boulders and crashing into small bathtub-like pools of swirling water, shaking the earth and sending great sprays of mist that brushed the faces of onlookers from far above. The Shad moved as a force through the valley like a thundering herd, all heavy hoofs and screams fleeing from some unseen predator. In its merciless rush, The Shad threw up waves of frothy water against the slabs, shooting bursts of droplets that suspended above the stream before free-falling. The Shad hurled on, roaring into a small canyon before suddenly hurling downward from sheer cliffs of rock—a waterfall pouring into a magnificent pool of churning water.

The rocks, the furious rush of water made fishing here difficult. Hiking down to the stream was all but impossible. As it was, every so often there came reports of a lost hiker or two. Inevitably, the body of an unlucky rock climber was found washed ashore farther downstream. For years, Jack had made clandestine trips here to this private piece of land to just sit and stare at the falls from far above and this hidden part of the Green Spring Valley, one of nature's more magnificent pieces of handiwork. Some nights he'd remain awake in bed, only to lull himself to sleep with the images and the sounds of the surging, roaring waters of The Flats. It was a place to come and ponder life's many riddles, a place for escape and dreams.

Of course, he had no illusions of being able to ever erect a cabin nearby. The fishing and hunting club members, comprised of mostly lawyers, doctors and other professional men of means, had control of vast acres of The Flats area. It was off limits to anyone else. The heavily posted dirt road leading up to the club made that clear. But the Flats covered a wide swath of real estate, and Jack knew heavily wooded sections of The

Shad well away from the club that provided enough cover to make for clandestine access to the stream. Intrepid anglers willing to hike a mile or so of the rocky, rugged mountain terrain could enjoy some of the finest fishing to be found on The Shad.

Soothsayer had taken Jack there years ago, and that first look at The Flats had done something to him. Perhaps once every few years, he'd make the tough hike into the canyon area to fish around the falls. All the time and effort to reach this special piece of water was always worth it. Unlike sections of The Shad that got heavy fishing pressure, the trout didn't easily spook here and were usually more than willing to grab flies thrown out to them. And there were some big beautiful trout too. Many of them could be found in the pools and riffles below the falls, waiting for the bugs that came drifting to them. The return of the Green Drake had made this area even more attractive for fly fishing. In his guiding trips up and down the stream since the comeback of the Green Drake, Jack had seen no greater concentration of the insects than in those waters below the falls.

And now, Adamly was eyeing this piece of real estate and wanted Jack to go partners with some folks. As much as Jack enjoyed having Adamly around and being charmed by the guy, he couldn't say Adamly was what could be described as trustworthy. Not that he completely held this character flaw against him.

How many times had Adamly strode into the bar flashing a thick roll of money with an offer to buy drinks for everyone in the bar?

"Musta been a good week in the lawyerin' world," Tar said.

"Must have been," Adamly responded, the corners of his mouth upturned in a smile that reminded Jack of some long-forgotten cartoon villain from his childhood who twirled a fiendish mustache with the ends of his long fingers.

There would follow brief talk of one property or other changing hands, a hefty profit, of course, for Adamly, but at a fair price, he assured Jack, for all parties involved.

Soothsayer found it appalling, even if a few lovely women catching wind of these conversations found it appealing. Jack never knew quite what to think. He was, after all, aware of his own transgressions in the business world.

One scheme Jack had concocted involved asking a deposit up front from clients he was to guide. It was simple in its manipulation. Clients paid a nominal fee of twenty dollars to reserve their day on the water. The full fee of one hundred dollars for a half day of guiding or one hundred and seventy-five for a full day was then paid by the client to Jack just prior to the two of them going out on the water. The deposit, of course, was to later be returned to the client. Jack knew that many clients never bothered asking for the deposit back. And if they didn't ask, well … he found no reason to remind them of the oversight. At the end of a few months, Jack could find himself pocketing an extra hundred dollars or two.

This little scheme didn't in the least make Jack feel guilty. He figured most of his clients had deep pockets. After all, anyone who could dole out the sort of money his guiding service demanded could afford to be swindled just a bit. And if it was a client who'd been snotty or rude to him, he took great satisfaction in cheating them out of a few extra dollars.

Jack couldn't imagine cheating any of this buddies or neighbors, however. The people around here who'd always been there to lend a hand, to pitch in when he needed his roof repaired or a new septic tank dug out, were wonderful folks. *His* kind of people. He could no more swindle them than he could cheat Soothsayer. As for Adamly, Jack had a strong suspicion the guy would sell out his own mother if there was something in it for him, and that made him uneasy.

Tar had found some cards and began a game of blackjack with Goldy. The game seemed to fascinate the girl. She didn't even notice Adamly slip off the stool next to her and plop himself on the stool next to Jack.

"You've been quiet so far today."

"I'm in deep thought," Jack said.

"That's a change."

"Hey. Give me credit. I'm no worse off in the brains department than that little number you brought in here."

Tar grinned. "Who? Goldy? Just a nice Catholic girl with a wonderful self-image."

"Yeah, as long as she's looking in the mirror. C'mon. Where did you find her? At the junior high?"

"Now. Now. Do I note a tad bit of jealousy coursing through those veins of yours Jack McAllister?"

"More than you'll ever know."

"Yeah. I heard it's been a while since you've been laid. What's the matter? The mountain maidens no longer cater to your every need and whim?"

"Everyone's a feminist any more. You know me. I'm a simple guy with simple needs."

"And a *simpleton*, I might add."

Jack decided to let that one go. He was too damn tired for clever repartee and to even try to engage in these verbal jousts with Adamly required a particularly clear head.

"So, what brings you in here today?" Jack asked. "You come in to make fun of us yahoots or out of some weird need to make my life miserable?"

"Make your life miserable? On the contrary. I've come to enrich your life. That is … if you're open to some financial opportunities."

Here it comes, Jack thought.

"Lay it on me."

"The fishing club has lowered its price. To a very affordable rate, I might add. They just wish to keep the club's building in place and retain fishing privileges."

"How about this guy? He comes in here, insults my intelligence, not to mention my well-earned reputation as a lady's man, then he springs this land deal on me."

Adamly grinned. "Okay. I take back the jab at your sexual prowess."

"That's better."

"As for the land deal, I'm hardly springing it on you."

"Okay, but who wants those snotty, elitist assholes around?"

Jack couldn't help but notice Adamly fighting a smile. When Adamly was around, he never let a chance go by without taking shots at the lawyers, the bankers, the money men. Adamly referred to his own disdain for these men as his "blue collar martyr complex," which always served as a bit of amusement between the two.

"Jack. Jack. These are reasonable people."

"Reasonable people? When was the last time you saw a lawyer do anything right by the common man?"

Adamly stroked his chin as if in deep thought. "Let's see. I suppose you got me there."

"Your ass. I never got you. *Ever.*"

It was true. Even in the old days, when he was a young struggling lawyer, he was one move ahead of everyone else. In the all-night poker games, it was Jack, Tar or one of their drinking buddies, who inevitably lost his shirt. Never Adamly. He always folded at just the right time or came up with the big hand when the pot grew the largest. Eventually, Jack had come to see that playing poker, for him at least, was another one of those losing prospects, especially when Adamly was involved. Playing on with the hope of emerging with that one big lucky hand wouldn't do.

As he had grown older, Jack had pretty much kept under control those outside influences, those vices that threatened to ruin the simple life he'd carved out for himself in the mountains. He stopped playing poker. He kept away from, or at a good distance, the stray women who wondered into the bar. Maintaining control. That's what it was all about.

"Let me buy you a beer," Adamly said.

"Oh sure. Get me loaded and then have me agree to your little land swindle."

"Jack. Just hear me out."

Adamly began twisting the rings on his fingers. Jack noticed one of the rings, studded with a diamond, sparkling from the sunlight shining through the front window of the Roll Cast.

"Okay counselor. Tell me, what makes this deal worth listening to."

"Let's just say Judge Garrity owes me a favor."

"Who in the hell's Judge Garrity?"

"Longtime veteran of the Williamsburg legal wars. His judgeship controls major interest in the property, but he's retiring at the end of this year and heading to his just reward: an oceanside condominium in Florida. Look, he's dying to sell. But if we don't jump at this, he'll find someone else."

Jack sat staring at Adamly. He knew Soothsayer wouldn't be keen on this offer, especially since it involved Adamly. Not that Soothsayer had to know. Still, he trusted the advice of his old fishing buddy.

"And you want to do what with this place? Tell me once again."

"Lodging. Rent out the rooms to hunters, anglers, vacationers. Nothing big. Just a small operation."

"That's it?" Jack said.

"That's it."

"Why don't you buy me that beer."

Chapter 7

While Jack was considering his options, a young man in a newsroom about thirty miles away sat before his computer terminal thinking.

Ron Noble had been a newspaper reporter for three years, and in that time, he'd accomplished nothing in his job that moved the earth and heavens. He had no beat, and the features and other assignments he drew were of the innocuous sort that called for little in the way of enterprise or investigative reporting. Not that his newspaper, *The Daily Record*, was a bellwether of hard-hitting journalism. A standing joke among some its more sophisticated readers was that *The Record* was nothing more than a tired rag that merely recorded what sources told its reporters.

Ron wanted desperately to change that. He felt it was time. But like a newly born creature, he was unsure of his first steps. Sometimes, he'd slip a little editorializing into his stories, but that was the extent of his attempts at rebellion and reform.

Ron had come to *The Daily Record* from the Midwest, and like many Midwesterners with ambition and a vision of changing the world, or at least being on the cutting edge of sweeping changes, he was painfully aware of his roots. He had chosen to exorcise his Middle America background and come East, where he was convinced things were happening. That he had landed in Williamsburg, a good two hundred miles from the glittering spires of Gotham, didn't greatly distress him. He felt that by pushing eastward he'd bettered his chances of eventually closing in on New York, or perhaps Washington, D.C., or even Philadelphia, cities where he knew the heartbeat of the news was fast-paced and where he could really test his reporting skills.

He had not been able to escape Indiana fast enough. His formative years as the son of an insurance agent and an efficient homemaker had been normal, his upbringing that of a wholesome middle-class boyhood—Boy Scouts, sports, church, honor roll student. In many ways, he was the typical Midwestern kid. But even as a boy he'd been fascinated by what was out there in the rest of the world.

As a teenager, he first became aware of New York through baseball. Unlike most of his baseball loving friends and acquaintances around his Indiana hometown who'd lived and died with the Chicago Cubs or White Sox just a state away, Ron developed a rooting interest in the New York Yankees. But he was more than just a baseball fan. He could play the game too. A marvelous hitter, he was always able to drive the ball farther than his teammates and most of opponents, who stuck Ron with the nickname Matty, after Hoosier native and Yankees star Don Mattingly. And although his ability on the ball field didn't bring baseball scouts panting to the doorstep of his split-level home in

Darcyville, he was good enough to grab a scholarship from a small college across the state.

Things went as planned in college, at least at first. He made the team as a freshman, and even led the club in home runs. In the classroom, he maintained a solid B-plus average in his first year. Baseball and his studies kept him busy. Because he was shy, he didn't get many dates, but he managed to join a few clubs–the Young Republicans among them.

He came home to Darcyville that summer as planned, earned a little extra money doing odd jobs and to keep his baseball skills sharp, joined an amateur team that played on Saturdays and weekday evenings. The league's teams were comprised of young men, most of them blue-collar workers of either marginal or above-average baseball skills, many of whom had rarely been out of Darcyville or had little illusion of escaping its confines. The team Ron joined, The Scabs, were a cut above the rest of the league. Most of the teams had perhaps one or two college players on their rosters, but The Scabs were managed by a part-time baseball scout named Jim Easley, who had recruited more than a half-dozen college players and other talented players from the area.

One of Ron's teammates that summer was a kid named Singleton. On a team loaded with good ballplayers, Singleton was easily the most talented. He was also the only black among a roster of white faces. Ron envied the skills Singleton brought to the ball field.

He ran like a gazelle and his power with the bat surpassed even Ron's. But Singleton didn't bring much passion to the game in which he seemed destined to shine.

From his center field position, he occasionally loafed after fly balls he could have easily caught. He often showed up to games late or not at all. He had a haughty manner about him that a few of his teammates came to despise. He was estranged from most of them and during games sat at the far end of the dugout, the heavy aluminum bat he referred to as "The Dark Beast, resting upright on the bench between his legs. When it came his turn to bat, he'd bring the bat close to his lips and whisper, "C'mon Beast."

Singleton selected Ron as one of the few people with whom he chose to converse. Ron, unlike many of his teammates, had welcomed him when he joined the club a few games into the season. His arrival had forced the team's longtime center fielder, an older man in his mid-thirties with diminishing skills, to the bench. Ron, being new to the team himself, felt a sort of kinship with Singleton.

Before games, he usually found himself standing next to Singleton in the outfield shagging batting practice fly balls. Ron came to learn that Singleton was from Chicago's South Side, and he was playing at the behest of Easley, who was always on the lookout for talent. Easley had come across Singleton whacking balls off the roof of a housing project during a recruiting visit to the city.

He badly wanted Singleton for his summer team and dangled before him the possibility of a professional contract. The catch was Singleton move to Darcyville, join his team, and to earn his keep, work that summer on a construction crew made up of Easley and some of his cronies. But things didn't go so well for Singleton at work. He'd been given the gopher tasks and more than once had been referred to as a "nigger" by one or two of the men. Singleton had hinted more than once to Ron of heading back to Chicago where "I belong."

"I don't fit in Whitey's world," Singleton said one evening as he shagged balls next to Ron in the outfield.

"Who's Whitey?" Ron asked, thoroughly puzzled.

Singleton dropped his glove and began laughing.

"You gotta be kiddin' dude."

"No. I'm not," Ron said, still confused.

"It's time we educate you my man."

Singleton smiled, shook his head and walked away.

The name Whitey played on Ron's mind. Throughout the game as he sat on the bench watching his teammates pound out hits or stood at his first base position pawing at the dirt with his cleats between pitches, he wondered: Who was this Whitey? Was it a foreman on the construction crew who was giving

Singleton a tough time? Then it dawned on him. Whitey was him, and it was all his teammates. In fact, Whitey comprised most of the American populace.

Ron would never admit it, but he always suspected he was a bit naïve about some matters, a pace or two behind his peers in aspects of worldly wisdom. He was, he realized, perhaps even the epitome of the square, small town Midwestern boy.

Before the next game, Singleton came up to him on the bench and dropped a copy of The *Autobiography of Malcolm X* on his lap. Ron quickly concealed the volume in his baseball bag he kept under the dugout bench. That night, in his bedroom where the walls were adorned with photographs of Major League baseball stars and pennants of Big Ten University gridiron teams, he looked over the volume. For the longest time, he sat there on the edge of his bed, his legs tingling, his stomach jumping, just staring at the title. With the book in his trembling hands he almost felt like a criminal hording stolen money.

There was something forbidden about the book. He recalled from high school certain titles that had been banned by the school board. Had this been among them? At the same time, there was something fascinating about the very front cover showing a bespectacled black man looking to convey powerful words of conviction to readers. He felt sure some rare, but valued knowledge could be found between its covers, words screaming for him to devour. And so, after locking his door, he began reading about the life of Malcolm X.

The literature was a revelation to Ron. He had never read anything so powerful or enlightening. He didn't necessarily agree with all the words put down by this fiery Civil Rights leader. Still, there was an important message here. For the first time, he began to look hard at his own life. Comparing his upbringing and background to that of Singleton, he realized the advantages he'd enjoyed. His eyes were beginning to see things in a different light; his mind was suddenly open for the first time to oppression. He wanted to discuss some of these things with Singleton. And so, he did. His teammate suggested he further his education by delving into the works of other black writers—Richard Wright and Ralph Ellison and James Baldwin.

By the time Ron returned to college that fall his mind was buzzing with new thoughts and an entirely unique perspective. There was another America out there, a society vastly different from his comfortable Midwestern upbringing. The fact that everyone in the country wasn't sharing in its vast economic riches gnawed at him, even disturbed him. He found himself feeling guilty for having been born into his middle-class life. He questioned his entire existence. His studies and baseball, a game he had always loved, no longer seemed all that important.

He'd sit in his dorm room watching the endless parade that passed for college life outside his window.

Students tossed Frisbees on the lawn and handsome, love-struck couples strolled across the campus, snuggling and embracing, exchanging dewy-eyed smiles. It seemed so many around him were oblivious to the big questions in life. Was anyone else considering these important social issues? In those first weeks of his returning to school, he was consumed by the need to discuss these thoughts hounding him.

One crisp autumn night, as he was walking across campus, he noticed a small gathering of students in front of a lecture hall. A long-haired youth was handing out pamphlets as a steady stream of students pushed their way into the building. Feeling more curious than anything, Ron fell into the throng, flashed his student identification card to a student usher, and made his way into the balcony.

The program that evening had already started. Down below him, a man was on the stage speaking. Ron had no idea who the person was. There was certainly nothing impressive about the guy. The plain-colored suit he wore seemed to hang somewhat on his lanky frame, and he spoke in a sort of droll monotone. He reminded Ron of a store clerk. And yet, his audience, which filled the auditorium, appeared rapt and attentive. And as Ron began to listen to the man's words, he soon found himself enthralled.

He claimed the country was run by corrupt and greedy politicians who were successful only in duping the American public into electing them into office year after year. And, they weren't working for the American public, despite what they told their constituents. Instead, they were puppets of powerful corporations, of money interests. The president and names of a few lawmakers Ron recognized came under fire. The government, the banks, the media, even academia were all part of the problem. Many of the students sitting there in the lecture hall, he made it clear, could become part of the problem as well as they took their places in the workplace in coming years.

"Are you a communist?" one student in the audience asked.

With a straight face, the man said he wasn't. He said he loved his country and only wanted to do what was right by it. He threw up a challenge to all the students: Do something now for your nation. Speak out. Challenge the status quo.

"But aren't there risks?" a voice inquired.

"Certainly, there are risks," he said. He offered himself up as an example. And with a slight grin he recounted how the U.S. government had targeted him as America's most dangerous man, that he'd followed by the FBI.

"What about when I need to get a job?" another student asked.

"Ask your prospective employer if you can bring your conscious to work with you," he responded with a straight face.

Laughs and guffaws followed, and then, more questions, including some silly ones. One student wanted to know if there was any truth to the rumor he still wore one of the numbers of pairs of shoes the Army issued to him when he was a soldier in the 1950s.

"The same ones," he said, lifting his right foot to display the sole of one of the shoes.

By the time the man left the stage, Ron had concluded that this remarkable individual was either the world's greatest charlatan or a crusader of heroic proportions, a figure who held so fiercely to his own uncompromising values that he had dedicated his life to reform. Outside the lecture hall, Ron picked up a pamphlet from off the ground, and by the light of an October moon, he looked over the literature. The plain-speaking man who had exhorted students to change America was Ralph Nader.

The name meant nothing to him, but over the next couple of days Ron spent much of his free time at the campus library digging deeply into this historic figure's past and writings. He was astonished to learn that an entire grassroots movement had been inspired by this man. Before Nader, consumer rights had been largely unheard of. A book he'd written on the automobile industry had introduced new laws designed to protect motorists. But what perhaps impressed Ron most of all was that Nader had renounced his own Ivy League background to take on these powerful institutions run by Harvard-trained lawyers and the like.

Ron had been looking for someone to articulate his own burgeoning ideas and feelings that had left him feeling so isolated from everyone and the seemingly carefree days of college life, and now here was this man who spoke up for so many people. The more he read of Nader and his accomplishments, the more fired up he was to do something. But where did one start? Here he was, at this college plunked down in Middle America, surrounded by youths from small towns and farms whose corn-fed values he felt more and more alienated from. The prospects of bringing about change seemed grim from this Midwest outpost.

He began to wonder if college was a mistake.

When the Thanksgiving holiday arrived, Ron boarded a bus, not for home but to Chicago where he found a cheap apartment room and took a job soliciting funds door-to-door for an environmental organization. Each afternoon, he'd report to the organization's downtown office and scan the literature about polluted streams or the devastation of clear-cut logging. Sometimes there was a pep talk from one of the managers. Ron would later learn these informal meetings were little different from the rallying cries sales managers gave to their underlings before sending them out on the road. And so, each day Ron and the other canvassers would then climb into a van and be driven out to the city's neighborhoods or to one of the bedroom communities to knock on doors.

He believed in the work. Day after day for several weeks, he dutifully reported to the job, listened to the talks exhorting him and other canvassers to raise money for the great cause. He grew excited of the prospect of getting behind a grassroots movement, that of doing his small part to save the world from environmental devastation. But he dreaded the door-to-door sales pitches he had to make. He simply could not get past his own shyness. He lacked the assertive, confident approach that such work demanded. When he repeatedly failed to reach his weekly sales quotas, the organization fired him.

It was January by then, and the cold winds coming off Lake Michigan were particularly frigid that winter. Needing money and feeling restless, he headed south to live with an uncle in Texas, taking a job as a security guard in Fort Worth. The mild winter climate was to his liking, and his job guarding homes in one of the city's most exclusive neighborhoods was an easy one. But it didn't feel right. The very idea that behind the doors of these mansions were oil barons and money makers living lives of privilege and wealth while others had nothing, or so much less, bothered him. By the summer, he was back at his boyhood home in Darcyville, disillusioned as ever about things and unsure about his future.

One day, he spotted an advertisement in the classified section of the local newspaper:

Looking for a MOVER AND SHAKER, Writing ability a must, College background helpful but not necessary. There was a phone number.

Out of curiosity as much as any other reason, Ron called the number. It turned out to be a job opening for a reporter at the *Phoenix Gazette*, a local weekly tabloid Ron had never heard of. Was he interested?

Ron hesitated. Newspaper reporter? A myriad of thoughts went through his brain as his hand held the telephone receiver. He was, in fact, a pretty good writer. The essays he'd written for his freshmen composition class had garnered him A's. Heck, it had been his best subject. He'd gotten a kick out of stringing words together. But a reporter? He had no experience at such a job. And didn't such a position require meeting people—all sorts of people—and in some cases, badgering them for information? God no. That wasn't for him. He'd seen those movies with the tough-talking reporters. He knew from his experience in Chicago that he was no people person. Heck, that supervisor back in Chicago told him he had needed to push people for sales.

He was about to tell the young woman on the phone: Thanks, but no thanks. But, as much to pacify his parents, who had been increasingly pressing him to go back to college or find a job, he agreed to go down to the place for an interview.

He didn't bother to put on a suit and tie for the meeting, instead opting for blue jeans and a t-shirt. He had already made up his mind that he didn't want to be a reporter. What was the point in trying to impress anyone? Since dropping out of college, the idea of wearing clothes more suited to insurance salesmen and bankers was repugnant to him anyway.

When he arrived at the newspaper, he was surprised to see, like him, everyone was casually dressed. The entire operation of *The Phoenix* was housed in a single upstairs room of a decrepit storefront in a rundown section of town.

Monica, the young assistant editor with whom he'd spoken on the phone the previous day, was there to greet him. She was a mild version of a punk rocker with a crazy orange hair-do and tattered blue jeans. Her easy smile and pleasant personality made him feel right at home. The room itself was drab, even seedy, with a moldy aroma. Ron couldn't help but be struck by the furnishings. It was an atmosphere with all the trappings of an underground operation run on a shoestring budget, a sort of raucous fraternity house trying to make a statement. Posters for Amnesty International, The Sierra Club and other liberal causes were plastered on the faded walls. There was little in the way of furniture, save for Monica's desk and a chair and desk in the corner where a young man was talking on the phone.

He was Burt, the newspaper's editor. At first glance, Burt looked every bit the nice young man who in fact had grown up middle class and happy in Peoria. He was soft-spoken with neatly trimmed short brown hair and a clean, athletic look about him. But the scrubbed, all-America image belied a young man with a hot fire in his belly.

There was work to do, he told Ron. Much work. Right here in Darcyville, people were going hungry to bed. Politicians were on the take, and landlords were ripping off the poor. He had been fighting tooth and nail with some of these bastards. Did Ron know that the school board took bribes from prospective teachers looking to land jobs?

He pushed a copy of *The Phoenix* across the desk toward Ron. The headline screamed at him: "Mayor to poor: SCREW YOU."

"The mayor wants to close down the city-run soup kitchen. He claims there's no money in the budget. So where does the city find the five thousand dollars to send him and some of his city cronies last winter to Honolulu for a municipal government seminar that was nothing more than an excuse for those fat cats to soak up some sunshine?"

Burt snatched the newspaper from off his desk and rattled it before Ron.

Ron grinned. "I never heard about that."

"Of course, you didn't," Burt said. "Do you think the *Daily Gazette* is going to write about it? My newspaper is the only one with the balls."

Burt's voice had grown more animated and loud. He rose from his seat and began walking about the room. He stopped at the single window overlooking the street. Burt squinted his eyes from the bright sunshine pouring through the window. For a few moments, he stood there peering outside.

He turned to face Ron. "If you're willing to take on these guys, I'd love to have you."

Ron was so excited he accepted the job on the spot. Years later, he had to laugh at his naiveté.

The Phoenix, he soon learned, was a ship treading water. The printing costs alone were sinking the newspaper deeper and deeper into a sea of red ink, forcing Burt to devote far too much time scrambling for advertisers to pay off the mounting debts. The paper's advertisers were hardly rolling in dough. The one or two health food stores and struggling defense attorneys placing ads in *The Phoenix* often paid their bills late, or not at all. The paper was distributed for free, making it completely dependent on its few advertisers. Finding businesses or organizations eager to place ads in a failing newspaper out of step with much of the conservative community it covered was a challenge.

Ron's paycheck reflected the fortunes of the paper. He earned barely above minimum wage, but he really didn't care. He was doing some stories, exciting ones, covering issues that he felt in some small way helped better the lives of some people. He managed to somewhat overcome an initial reluctance to confront officials. Naturally shy and brought up to respect authority, he suddenly realized what a kick it could be to challenge it.

Early on, he did several stories on municipal waste. In one article, he exposed city employees' use of government vehicles for personal use. He probed the school system for nepotism and employees who were collecting paychecks for doing virtually nothing. An attendance monitor related to the school superintendent hired at fifty-thousand dollars per year to keep down school truancy was himself frequently absent from work.

The work was by turns rewarding and frustrating. He would chase stories only to find no one willing to talk to him. Public officials were reluctant to allow him to probe government records. But he liked making a small difference, and he found it a real kick to see his byline over a story. Never mind that the newspaper was not widely read. In fact, it was vastly ignored by the greater populace of the city.

"You know you're doing something right when the movers and shakers of this town call you up to scream at you," Burt said with a sly smile.

It was true. Here Ron was, this young guy, making life miserable for the power brokers, the scoundrels. *The Phoenix* was everything he'd been searching for, offering him a tool he could use to carve out some sort of meaning in his life. Unfortunately, he was out of a job after six months.

Incredibly enough, Burt, the muckraking journalist who had exposed the crooks and the miscreants and the liars, was himself a bit of a scoundrel. Ron and others found themselves not getting paid a month's worth of work, not because the paper couldn't afford to meet payroll as they'd been told by Burt. Rather, Burt had siphoned off their earnings for himself. No sooner was Burt exposed for his shenanigans when he fled town, and the paper shut down.

And so began a four-year odyssey of newspaper work that took Ron from Indiana to Ohio to western Pennsylvania and finally eastward to *The Williamsburg Daily Record*. During those years he would find no job even remotely rewarding as his days at *The Phoenix*. He wondered if he ever would. *The Phoenix*, for all its problems, had been this incredible training ground for practicing real journalism. Other papers shied away from the muckraking reporting. Editors such as Burt, he found to his chagrin, were a rare breed, and newspapers willing to stick their necks out for the greater good of the public were perhaps even harder to find. Employee cutbacks at the last two newspapers where he'd worked had prevented him from doing any real enterprise reporting. "Just give 'em the facts," he'd been told. "We don't have the resources for investigations."

As he sat at his desk in the newsroom of *The Daily Record* on this spring day, he was not so much engaged in his work as contemplating his next career move. Where was he to go? What would he do? He was a college dropout who'd done virtually nothing but newspaper work. If only he could recapture the excitement from his days at *The Phoenix*. But that all seemed such a distant memory.

He had a council meeting tonight, a school board meeting the following evening. It was all he was doing anymore. Going to meetings and writing about tax hikes and budgets and potholes and paving projects and minor squabbles over school curriculums. Often, he felt like nothing more than a stenographer. Was this to be his fate?

"Noble? What are you working on?"

Gene Risky, his craggy-faced editor, stood over his desk.

Ron could feel conflicting emotions of trepidation, excitement and comic relief. With Risky, you were never quite sure what to expect.

To most reporters at *The Daily Record* he was a throwback, Hollywood's version of the short-tempered, hard-drinking, no-nonsense editor. Newly hired reporters at *The Daily* Record were especially wary of the grumpy, middle-aged editor. And for good reason. Risky seemed to take sadistic glee in testing those reporters who had chosen journalism as a career. More than a few had given up the high calling of journalism for good after failing Risky's famous initiation rite. Before even being hired, every prospective reporter was sent to the local police station to gather news. There, he or she was met by a burly six-foot, six-inch slab of meat named O'Farrell who oversaw law enforcement duties.

"Who the fuck sent you here," O'Farrell would scowl at the reporter.

"I'm a reporter from *The Daily Record.*"

"That liberal rag. I wouldn't wipe my ass with that newspaper. Get the hell out of here."

And if the reporter did flee the premises without scanning the police log for news, Risky decided that person would never work at *The Daily Record.*

If, like Ron, they stood up to O'Farrell, Risky felt they at least had "half a chance to be a reporter."

Some found Risky's ways hard to take. In addition to his occasional temper outbursts, he had about him a cynical outlook formed by too many years of journalism. And his bawdy humor and off-color jokes, many of them with ethnic references, were not always well received. In his defense, he called himself an equal opportunity bigot.

"Hell. I've had Chinks here working for me, darkies, wetbacks, dagos, krauts, mics, kikes, you name it. Still looking to hire a Jap." Risky referred to himself as a Jew boy with parts of Cherokee, Irish and German blood coursing through my veins."

"Hell, my mother took one look at my sorry mongrel ass coming out of her and decided to leave me on a doorstep."

And Ron realized early on that some of Risky's cruelest jokes were often directed at himself, an apparent attempt to wipe out the sadness of his life.

An orphan, Risky had come up hard. Undersized even as a kid, he wasn't much good at sports. Early on, he'd found that only shouting or pushing his way into the midst of things could get him anywhere. "I'm the classic fuckin' case of a guy suffering from short man's disease."

He'd dropped out of school at sixteen then wondered south from the orphanage in Albany to New York City, more out of curiosity about the big city than for any other reason. He was fascinated by the frenetic pace, the crowds and the skyscrapers looming about him on the island of Manhattan. Strangely, he felt right at home. At the time, it was late winter, and with just a few dollars in his pocket and needing a place to stay, he wondered into a building. Little did he know that this crumbling structure was home to one of the numerous daily newspapers then operating in the big city. The night doorman, who took pity on him and allowed him to spend the night in the lobby, dropped the information that they were looking for copy boys upstairs.

He didn't have the faintest idea what a copyboy was, but the next morning he took the elevator to an upper floor to investigate. As he later recalled to Ron, "It was as if I'd died and gone to heaven."

One look at the newsroom with its furious pace, ringing phones and desks where reporters and editors in white shirts sat, their neckties askew, some of them shouting into phones, and he knew it was where he wanted to be.

He soon pushed his way into a reporting job. In those days if you showed a bit of spunk you could do that, he said. He found he had a natural flair for writing, although as he admitted even now, "I was no damn Hemingway. Hell, we had guys in that newsroom who wrote damn near as good as Papa himself. Drank like the old bastard too."

The job itself suited him just fine. In those days, when more than a half-dozen dailies were putting out multiple editions, the job had called for aggressive, often cutthroat reporting which suited young Risky just fine. It was on-the-job training. A mad scramble to a fire in Brooklyn in the afternoon, an interview with a shady underworld figure in the evening over a drink. A job of excitement and passion. New York had it all, and Risky couldn't get enough of the job or the city in those days.

"I got to know it all–Manhattan, Brooklyn, The Bronx, Queens–and all the crazy denizens of that wonderful town. From the bums in The Bowery to the Park Avenue swells. That was what was so great about the job. One day you might be talking to the mayor, the next day to some bartender or Teamster in Flatbush. We rattled some cages in those days too. Don't think we didn't."

Risky and three other reporters on the newspaper came to be known as the "Fabulous Four", a tribute to their investigative reporting skills, particularly in the uncovering of corruption in city hall.

"We didn't clean up the city. No way. You can't shovel all the shit by hand out of a landfill. But we grabbed a few fuckers by the balls."

Hardball reporting, late-night drinking binges at the Lion's Head Bar in Greenwich Village, heady times for a young reporter in the world's greatest city. But it wasn't to last. Newspapers were drowning in red ink. Many of them closed, including Risky's. Newspaper jobs dried up. Risky was forced to leave the city he'd come to love for parts unknown. Learning of an opening for an editor at a small town daily in Pennsylvania, Risky applied for the job and got it.

"Now, I'm nursemaid to a bunch of wet-behind-the-ears rookies who don't know a good lead from a shit."

But Risky's problem wasn't really with the reporters, who were more educated if not as street smart as some of his old colleagues he'd broken in with back in his own reporting days. Risky's beef was with the reporting itself. Blood and guts journalism was out. For a time, Risky had overseen an eager, talented staff of reporters who'd taken up Risky's down-in-the-gutter style of journalism. Awards had been many, and for a time, *The Daily Record* was a force in the community, but with the 1980s came new ownership, a corporate giant that bought out the single family who'd run the newspaper for three generations. It ushered in a new philosophy. No longer was Risky given free rein to run the newsroom as he saw fit. The new owners simply did not want to ruffle the feathers of advertisers.

It hardly sat well with Risky who occasionally did his best to shove controversy to the front page. Many were the times in recent years when he found himself being called on the carpet for embarrassing one of the city's respected businessmen or pols. His rebellious acts grew fewer. And as the old editor edged closer to retirement, he was increasingly shutting himself off from reporters, closing the door to his office, and drinking.

Ron was surprised to see Risky looming over his desk on this morning. Although the two of them had gotten along well, it seemed to Ron that it had been weeks since they'd said more than a few words to each other.

"Ya gotta minute Noble?"

Risky appeared uneasy. The ever- present cigar shifted from one side of his mouth to the other. He used his stubby fingers to push back the gray strands of disheveled hair on his head. These impromptu meetings with Risky were not altogether rare. Occasionally, Risky would call Ron into his office, but never to be bawled out for some screw-up in a story or to go over some important aspects of an article. If Risky had something to say to a reporter he made a beeline to his or her desk and took care of business on the spot. No formal meetings or office memos for Risky.

When Ron was called into Risky's office, it was often to act as a sounding board for the editor's problems, concerns, his gripes with management. It was a role Ron had come to accept, at first reluctantly, but later as a badge of honor. No other reporter, Ron learned, was privy to this often volatile, but interesting man's concerns and frustrations. There had grown a respect between the two—the ambitious young reporter and the gruff, sharp-minded old editor.

Ron followed him into his cluttered office. Ron never failed to be amazed at the great heap of disorganization that served as Risky's office. Risky sneered at any suggestion of getting his house in order. He laughed at filing systems, calling them the bane of good journalism. Reporters like Ron, who kept Rolodex systems and little black books to keep track of meetings and sources, often took a good ribbing from Risky. "You wanna be neat, you wanna be organized, you're in the wrong business kids. Go take up bookkeeping. Anything you need to remember ought to be here," he said, holding up a small tattered notebook, "or right up here," he added, pointing an index finger at his head.

"Shut the door behind you Noble."

Ron and the old editor sat down facing each other across Risky's cluttered desk.

"I suppose you know that the paper's in trouble."

Ron nodded. He'd seen the pink slips going out. More and more jobs at the paper were becoming part-time gigs. A few other slots had gone unfilled. But then again, rumors that *The Daily Record* was losing money had been circulating since he'd been hired nearly two years ago. It was the nature of the newspaper business anymore.

"But that ain't why I called you in here. It's only a prelude to what I've got to say. I'm getting out too. Call it early retirement. They're dangling some money for me to take. A lump sum. If I don't grab it now … well …"

Ron didn't know what to say. The prospect of retirement to him seemed foreign, something reserved for feeble old hands who were of little use any longer. For Risky, retirement seemed absurd. Risky had no children from a long, but now dissolved marriage. *The Daily Record* was his life. Every morning he was in his office, long before the other editors and reporters arrived, and often still there late at night when others were gone.

"It's time," Risky said, shifting uneasily in his chair and staring at Ron, his cigar pasted between the thick lips of a face that seemed to show the ravages of too many deadlines, long late nights and no small amount of booze.

"Well … I guess if that's what you want to do," Ron said.

"Hell man. That ain't what I want to do. Don't ya see? They got me by the balls."

And now Risky stood up—slowly. He removed his cigar from his mouth and flourished it about.

"These assholes who took over have wanted me out of here since they arrived."

"They wouldn't dare fire you," Ron said.

A faint smile appeared on Risky's face. For a few moments, he stood in the corner of his office staring through the glass looking out at the newsroom, the same newsroom he'd ruled over for the past thirty-odd years, where so many reporters had learned the rudiments of the trade from him, many of whom left *The Daily Record* for bigger and better things, their bylines appearing in national publications.

Years earlier, right after the take-over, the corporation had placed a full-page advertisement in the paper announcing Risky's retirement and the hiring of a new editor, a younger man who'd been groomed at a smaller company paper to take his place. It didn't sit well with some of the reporters and other editors, who threatened to walk off the job if their tough old boss editor was removed from his rightful position. The corporate people backed off, and Risky's job was saved, but the men in the suits at the downstate office continued to do what they could to make his life miserable. Controversial stories were killed time and again. And repeatedly, Risky would rail against management putting the bottom line above good journalism.

"Yeah. My days are numbered. Next month, I'll be gone. Another tiny blimp in the annals of journalism." Risky turned to Ron. "Screw it. There ain't no reason why I can't go out in a blaze of goddamn glory." A sly, mischievous grin appeared on the editor's face. "How would you like to go down with me Noble?"

Risky leaned against a wall of his office with his arms folded. His tiny cigar was nearly lost in the full-blown, maniacal grin. Ron felt his heart skip. This was Risky at his most interesting and complex. Sullen, pensive and resigned one moment, effervescent and calculating in the next moment.

"What do you have in mind?"

"Look. It's up to you. I wouldn't ask you to risk a job that meant much to you. Then again, the reasons why a talented guy like yourself with the potential to showcase his work in far bigger arenas would remain in this burg is another question."

And there it was: A challenge had been issued, and the praise quickly given. The wily editor at his best. Still, Ron found himself fighting an embarrassed grin, the same stupid, unwanted and lopsided grin that ultimately appeared whenever Risky praised his talents. They both knew what was coming next. Risky had taken Ron down this road before.

"What story do you want me to dig up that has absolutely no chance of getting published in this newspaper?"

Risky sat down in the swivel chair behind his desk.

"Have I told you that I've always liked you boy?"

PART II

Chapter 8

Another season of the Green Drake Hatch had nearly arrived. During the five years that had passed since its rebirth at the Shad, the Green Valley emerged as one of those must-fish streams for fly fishermen. Anglers who were on the water when the insects filled the air just before dusk in such great quantities were in for an experience. The trout swimming throughout the stream's now popular fishing waters had grown fatter and in greater numbers.

The Green Drake Hatch was a time Jack had grown to dread. The first couple of years the hatch had been fine. He had enough business guiding clients in that two-week period of the hatch to pay off some creditors and keep him stocked in bamboo rods. He even had some time to get in some of his own fishing. But by the third year of the hatch, it was chaos.

As far as Jack was concerned, it was an article appearing in a national fishing publication that had really ignited the invasion. An April edition of the magazine had told of vast numbers of the Green Drakes taking flight during late May at the Shad. The story itself had mixed facts with fiction. There was the suggestion that the Green Drakes had been present in small secluded areas of the stream for many years, but that some local unnamed fly fishermen over time had somehow mysteriously been able to keep the hatch secret from others. Like many good stories bathed in legend and mystery and no small degree of controversy, it carried with it a degree of truth. There had, in fact, over the years been reports of a Green Drake Hatch at the Shad, although, as far as Jack and Soothsayer were concerned, those stories were always a lot of crap.

Jack had to give the writer of the angling publication credit. He'd done his research. An entomologist told him that a Green Drake Hatch appearing in such prolific numbers was indeed a remarkable event of nature, and was highly unlikely to suddenly appear in great abundance after such an apparent long absence. A few nationally renowned fly fishermen supported that view, and to further pave the way for the invasion sure to come, told of the difficulty and unpredictability of fishing over the hatch. One likened trying to catch trout during the hatch to that of chasing "alluring and elusive women."

Competent and experienced fly fishermen like nothing better than a challenge, and now, here was this heretofore, unknown stream in a wilderness area full of fat trout and a prolific hatch that had a touch of mystery about it. Well, it was just too much. Jack knew once the more expert fly fishermen began visiting the stream, many other anglers were sure to follow. That Jack and Soothsayer had both politely refused to grant interviews for the piece only added to the Shad's controversy and allure and now legendary status.

It was on that Friday just before the Memorial Day holiday, the eve of the now traditional kick-off of the expected Green Drake Hatch. Jack was sitting at his fly-tying table, working on the wings of a Green Drake.

It was dawn, and he was up early as usual to attend to the million things he had to do. He had clients lined up for the next three weeks, most of whom were hoping to get in on the Green Drake action. And that meant there were hundreds of flies to be tied. Beyond that, there were errands to run, last-minute preparations, including phone calls to make. So many of the clients expected him to get back to them with an update of stream conditions. After all, it was good business. Unfortunately, conditions couldn't have been better. It had been a spring of just the right amount of rain. Daytime temperatures in recent days had been about normal. The Shad was running cool and at a perfect flow for the trout for this time of year.

The weekend called for near perfect weather— sunny days with temperatures in the mid-70s, followed by chilly evenings. Jack made daily recordings of the water temperature and in recent days it had checked in at 63 degrees. The trout could be expected to be active and rising in the evening. More importantly, the first Green Drakes of the season had been coming off the Shad down at the Bend just the evening before. Yes. The Shad was in great shape for wonderful fishing. But as usual, with the holiday weekend now here, there'd be too many fishermen out on the water, and Jack could foresee the inevitable problems.

Most newcomers to the Shad had only the slightest notion of what they were up against during the Green Drake Hatch. With the arrival of so many fishermen, it was important for an angler to select a prime spot on the stream hours before the hatch began. Too many of his clients either expected Jack, as a guide, to have a spot reserved for them. And, they didn't realize how utterly frustrating the Green Drake Hatch could be even for the most expert of fly-fishermen.

The Shad had always been a great stream for other spring insect hatches as well—the Sulphur, the Grey Fox, the March Brown—and often when fishermen saw the trout rising in vast numbers, they just assumed it was for the Green Drakes. One particularly disagreeable client who was having no luck at all latching onto trout while using a Green Drake had ignored all Jack's instructions in switching to a Sulphur. He continued coming up with frustration, and to make matters worse, insisted on staying on the stream until nearly midnight without catching any fish.

Jack had his vision of the perfect client. He was a knowledgeable fly-fisherman and a fine fly-caster, but free of the stubborn or egomaniacal tendencies that prevented him from taking advice and readily learning the intricacies of fishing the Shad. Once in a blue moon, that client came to him. And it ultimately made for a fine experience. But oh God it was rare.

By noon, Jack had tied his last Green Drake of the morning. He figured to wrap up the day's fly-tying with some sulphurs and caddises. Hell, he thought, maybe some of these idiots will be willing to try one or two of those flies.

He gazed out the window of his cabin. It was a fine day all right. He hadn't yet gotten around to putting in the screens in the windows, but even with the window down he could all but taste the fresh spring air. In seasons long past, the familiar scent of pine and the maples bursting with the full flower of their leaves had left him dizzy with joy. A few robins were chasing each other beneath the rhododendron next to the stream. A couple of young men looking like models for an Orvis catalogue walked briskly past his window, attired in expensive looking fly-fishing gear—tight neoprene waders, olive green vests, the polished wooden handles of nets dangling at hips, their graphite rods glistening in the sun. He paused to watch them disappear through the rhododendron and onto the stream.

Yeah. It was going to be a fine day, he thought with a groan.

Jack checked his itinerary. He kept track of all his guiding client appointments in a large black log book. He was booked for every damn day for the next three weeks, save for Tuesday. His first clients were set to arrive about 3 o'clock. Tom Wilson and Maria Beers from Philly. Shit. He'd forgotten all about the fact that he was launching three weeks of hell with this pair.

He didn't know either of the two, but he had a pretty damn good idea what he'd be up against. Boyfriend drags the little honey who doesn't know shit about fly-fishing up here from the city for a weekend getaway. In the first hour, the boyfriend who barely can use a fly rod himself, thrusts the girlfriend upon him to teach her the intricacies of a successful dry fly cast. That failing, the boyfriend, all too anxious to catch fish, loses patience, and ultimately, all the dirty laundry from a not-so-wonderful relationship gets thrown out there on the stream.

Well, they had paid the two-hundred dollar guiding fee up front. At least, he wouldn't be fighting to get money from another well-heeled client.

Jack turned back to his fly-tying vice. With scissors, he snipped the end of the thread from one last fly. He turned the vice, carefully removing the fly from it to place the bug with the others on the table.

He slumped in his chair. He was tired already. Another night of just four hours sleep. The night before, he'd been in bed by ten o'clock determined to get some good shut eye. But then he'd tossed and turned and been unable to drift off to sleep. By midnight, he was up tying flies. It was only after he'd collapsed right here at the fly-tying table, that he'd finally felt ready for bed.

And then, the dream. The recurring strange dream. A huge rainbow trout leaping from a pool of the Shad and gulping a fly. But this was not a fly out of Jack's usual repertoire. It resembled a crumpled five-hundred-dollar bill. Jack set the hook, and in the next instant he saw the green and white fly lodged in the corner of the fish's mouth. The trout, with a single furious and frightening glance at Jack, heaved and leaped from the water, and with a thunderous splash, threw its great girth upward before streaking like a bullet downstream. The fish was the biggest and most spectacular trout Jack had ever seen. The bright crimson stripe down its silvery flanks glowed brightly, the black spots dotting its body flashing like neon lights. And Jack wanted this fish. Oh, how he wanted it. But it was soon clear to Jack that he was under the spell of something powerful.

Line ripped from his reel, but Jack could do nothing to bring his hands to work either the reel or the rod. And when he tried to run after the fish, his legs were useless to him. At the head of some riffles, the trout rose and pranced like a ballerina upon the surface, blood dripping from the corner of its mouth where the fly remained embedded. Sharp bicuspids flashed a smile at Jack, the eyes of the trout blinked mischievously, like those of a gambler with a winning hand, and then the trout turned and tore off for some rapids. Jack held furiously to his rod, bent like a horseshoe to the ground. Far downstream, the heavy trout leaped again, turned and called to Jack in a mocking tongue indecipherable to him. It tore through a boulder-strewn area of the stream, and snapped the line from Jack's reel, free now, laughing like the cruelest of Gods.

By four a.m. he was wide awake. He was still in his clothes from the previous day. Too dog-tired to get out of them. With a sigh, he rose from the table and trudged to the bathroom. Getting out of his clothes still reeking of the stream, he went to the mirror. Fully naked now, the image staring back at him in the mirror brought it all home. He was, he thought, nothing more than a middle-aged, sloppy guy gone slightly to fat. The fact that he hadn't shaved in days, let alone run a comb through his hair lent him the appearance of some reclusive mad woodsman. Or his damn father. A chilling thought. Still, he could see the similarities.

"Fat, fucking slob," he screamed at the image.

He grabbed the flesh just above his hip. What was the old saying: Pinch an inch. "Hell, pinch six inches," he said.

His jowls were even beginning to sag. At least he still had his hair, even if more gray was getting in there. Not a trace of baldness though. Yeah, there was one thing good to say about the McAllister genes. Drinkers, womanizers and brawlers. But hairless? Never.

Jack gave his full, unkempt head of hair a few loving pats. Women had always liked his hair. Running their long nails through it as he danced them drunkenly around the saw-dusted floorboards to the cacophony of a country western tune from the Roll Cast's blaring jukebox. He always kept it long, the locks just brushing his shoulders.

He stood before the mirror for a few moments, patting his hair and then studying the fleshy region of his face around his chin. And then he moved the palm of his hand over his chest and across his shoulders and down his arms. The scars were there, nasty reminders of a barroom fight or two and evidence of tumbles he taken in The Shad, were laid bare on his shoulders and arms.

During his years of fishing, he'd collected a cracked rib, wrenched knees, twisted ankles and the most debilitating injury of all—a screwed-up elbow from a nasty spill near some rocks down by The Bend. He still had that gap on his elbow from the ill-advised surgery he'd undergone to fix some ligament damage. Damn elbow still didn't feel quite right. For a moment, he studied the centipede-like markings on his arm and with the ends of his fingers followed its course from one end to the other. The quack who'd performed the surgery had severed some nerves and he still had no damn feeling in that area. That's when he felt the lump.

It was a small egg-shaped bump more than anything, no bigger than a peanut really. But it was there, under the skin in the funny bone area. Initially, he thought it was a huge pimple. He'd had those before. Painful little critters that he always squeezed open or lanced with a needle and then watched in sheer delight as the pus oozed forth like lava from a volcano. But this was different. No soreness at all. He moved his arm and stretched it over his head. The usual twinge in the elbow was there but nothing more. Funny what you could find with a little probing and prodding. He gave the bump a final probing with his fingers and got into the shower.

Chapter 9

The weekend rush had begun. Over at the Roll Cast, cars, pickup trucks and four-wheel drive vehicles were parked around the building, many of them with out-of-state license plates.

Inside, the bar was lined with an odd mixture of regulars and fly-fishermen, many of whom were there specifically to fish the Green Drake Hatch. Most of the few tables or booths were filled as well. Tar was rushing from behind the bar to the kitchen to relay food orders and bring drinks to patrons. Back in the kitchen, Jack spotted Tar's round wife, Fay, who often showed up in a pinch.

Jack figured to have a long wait to get a bite to eat on this day. But he had other more pressing concerns than his lunch. He remembered he hadn't gotten around to patching that hole in his waders. The damn waders had begun leaking this week and he'd intended to glue them before the weekend onslaught of anglers.

He and Adamly spotted each other at the same moment. The wily lawyer was at a table against the wall, dressed for fishing, which meant the very finest in fly-fishing attire—expensive neoprene waders, a vest straight from the Orvis catalogue and a landing net polished and shined. With a wide grin, he called Jack over. Jack saw he was sitting with someone, a young guy, an unfamiliar face.

"You're just the guy we're looking for," Adamly said. "Jack McAllister. Meet Ron Noble. Ron's a reporter for *The Daily Record.*"

Oh shit, thought Jack. What the hell's this all about? With Adamly you just never knew.

Jack shook his hand and sat down beside Adamly. "I was just telling the good reporter here about this great paradise we have up here," Adamly said.

Jack was vaguely aware of the briefcase snapping shut.

"It is really beautiful. I've never been this far north in the state," Noble said. "And this place, I guess this is what you'd call rustic." He began looking around the room now, his eyes taking special note of the large Brown Trout mounted above the bar.

Jack eyed the guy. He seemed like a nice, clean-cut young fella, not much different from some of the well-heeled fly-fishermen that invaded the area. He looked fit and trim and healthy enough, in a hit-the-gym workout kind of way. Probably a jogger.

"You from around here?" Jack asked.

"Indiana."

"Ron's a Hoosier. Hails from that grand republic of the prairie."

"So, are you writing an article on the Green Drake Hatch?" Jack asked.

And right away, Jack could see this guy didn't know a Green Drake from a caddis fly.

"What's that?"

Jack looked from the reporter to Adamly. "Isn't that why he's here?"

A strange grin creased Adamly's face. "Ron's what you call a features writer. Likes to get a feel for a place. Take in the ambience, talk it up with some of the local folk and put together an article."

"Actually, that's partly right Mr. Adamly. I did want to get a feel for the place. For example, I was wondering how you feel about the development of the area."

"Development?"

"We have reason to believe that big plans are being considered for land just to the south of here," he said.

Adamly raised a brow. There was a twinkle in his eye.

"And what gave you that idea?" Jack asked.

Who was this guy? Jack thought. I've lived here half my life and I don't know anything about development.

He looked at Adamly, who held up his hands.

"I've been trying to tell the gentleman Jack. I don't know anything about this. Why, development is the last thing we want up here in God's country. It's the very scourge to everything we people up here stand for."

Jack wondered where the "we" suddenly came from. While it was true, Adamly spent a lot of time up here, hunting and fishing in a half-assed kind of way— and making money off the good folks in dire need of legal services—he didn't live here for God's sake.

And now the reporter grew earnest. Out of his pocket he grabbed a document of some sort. He placed it on the table and pushed it toward the lawyer.

"Do you know anything about this?"

Adamly brought reading glasses up to his eyes and leaned his head down to scan the document. Jack looked as well. There was writing and horizontal lines running up and down both sides of the document. And now Jack concluded they were looking at recent deed transactions. The reporter used his index finger to trace a single line from the left to the right side of the paper:

The Shad Fishing and Hunting Club to The Green Valley Landowners Association Inc.

"What I want to know is who represents The Green Valley Landowners Association Inc.?" Noble asked.

Adamly's now steely eyes peered over the reading glasses and narrowed in on the reporter.

"I haven't the foggiest notion. It could be that club wants to subdivide some land and is looking for a buyer."

Adamly looked suddenly confused.

"But it's a done deal. Mr. Adamly. It's right here on the deed transaction. And you're the attorney of record for the hunting club."

Adamly leaned back in his chair before coming forward to fix Noble with an appraising smile. He glanced at Jack.

What gives? Jack thought. Adamly had come to him about going partners with that piece of property. Now this?

"Ha. Ha. Okay," Adamly said. "I see you're a good reporter. You went into the courthouse. You checked over land transactions. You poked around and asked some questions. Bravo. Take it from this seasoned barrister, there's a lot of interesting information to be gleaned from the musty morgues of that courthouse."

"What the hell's the deal?" Jack asked. "And what's the Green Valley Landowners Association?"

"Who knows? It's really not that important."

Adamly waved a single dismissive hand at the document.

And now the reporter trained his eyes on Jack. "*You've* never heard of this group Mr. McAllister?"

"Hell no."

"It's really curious," Noble said, scratching his head.

He used an index finger to trace the printed transaction on the document. It's a lot of land, and a lot of money too. Two hundred acres and two-and-a-half million dollars."

Noble shook his head.

Jack recalled a few years back when Harley Johns found it was time to give up his two-pump gas station about twenty miles away down at the cross roads. He'd made what seemed like a killing on that property. Rumor had it that the owners of that convenience store chain had given him something like fifty thousand dollars for that little piece of land. But two-and-a-half million dollars? Were there some grand plans for that land near The Flats?

"What gives Adamly?" Jack asked.

Adamly cleared his throat. He smiled at Jack, then at Noble. "This land we're talking about is, for all intents and purposes, in the middle of nowhere."

Adamly suddenly had a pen in his hand. He grabbed a napkin from off the table and proceeded to quickly draw up a diagram on it. It included the fishing club, the river flowing past and the surrounding land. "The only road going into there is a lousy, one-lane dirt road," he said as he drew a line on his little map to signify the road. He leaned back and looked down at the drawing.

"Two-and-half million dollars Adamly," Jack said.

Adamly held up two palms. "Land isn't cheap."

"Two-and-a-half million dollars," Jack repeated.

"Hey. These fishing and hunting club members are professionals … doctors and lawyers … men of means. They're not going to sell for nothing."

"Why are they selling at all?" Noble asked.

"They're retired old men mostly. Hell, half of these guys can't even get it up anymore, let alone get out to the woods and the stream to hunt and fish. They're ready to sell."

"I don't buy it," Jack said. He looked at Adamly, now with his arms crossed and smiling back at him.

Jack insisted that Adamly stop his BMW along the dirt road. Otherwise, the lawyer would have driven right up to the front of the club. The road was private, and the land heavily posted, but both Adamly and Jack well knew that club members never minded people using the road if they kept their distance from the large, two-story log building. There was rarely anyone around the place anyway. Even on this holiday weekend no vehicles were parked around the place.

The three of them got out of Adamly's car. For a long time, they stood looking around them at the land, at the hills beyond.

"The stream runs right along there," Jack said, turning to Noble before pointing to the line of trees running behind the club.

The three of them moved to the right of the building toward the stream. It was an open field and easy walking, despite the knee-high grass. Before the Shad even came into view, its roaring sound called to them.

"What is that?" Noble asked as he came to a stop to listen.

That's the Shad," Jack said.

"You mean the creek?"

Jack nodded.

"It's really remote, but I suppose I can imagine someone wanted to develop it. I mean, it's so beautiful out here," Noble said, looking around him.

"It sure is beautiful," Jack said. His stomach felt queasy.

"Gentlemen. Gentlemen. Who said it's being developed?"

"But the deed Mr. Adamly?"

"A land transaction. That's all it is."

Just above the soft roar of the creek, the unmistakable sound of a door slamming came from the rear of the building, and then, footsteps drawing closer to the three men. An old man, slightly stooped, his head lowered, made his way in a slow gait toward them.

"Judge Garrity," Adamly said. "And how are you?"

The old man brought up his eyes to Adamly and allowed himself a smile before proceeding toward the trio.

He extended a hand to Adamly and the two shook hands.

"No court today Mr. Adamly?" he said.

"Not today judge. It's my day off."

"Ah … and you're looking to get in some fishing too, I see," he said. He turned to Jack and the reporter. "Judge Lou Garrity," he said, shaking hands with them.

"So," the judge said, looking now at Adamly. "What have you heard?"

Adamly looked with puzzled eyes at the judge. "I … what do you mean?"

Jack could see Adamly biting down on his lip and shuffling his feet as he stared at the ground. Clearly, he was uncomfortable.

"I'm hearing a golf course." The judge slowly turned to take in the two-story cabin before them. "And this …. He gestured with a single hand at the building. "This will surely make for a grand hotel."

Jack stared at Adamly. What the hell? he thought.

Chapter 10

Jack usually met his clients down at the Roll Cast. It usually worked out fine that way. The store was in walking distance of some good holes along the Shad and his clients who were willing to stay in the cheap but clean rooms Soothsayer rented out, found it most convenient.

Jack had returned to the store in plenty of time to meet with Martin and Missy. He had Tar pour him a draft beer before he retreated to the porch to sit on the wooden steps leading up to the store's entrance. The time had been set for two o'clock. The plan was to get out on the water well before the Green Drake Hatch kicked off in the evening, maybe try grabbing some trout on some nymphs down at any one of the holes or possibly to explore one of the Shad's feeder streams.

The tributaries were narrow, fast-running bodies of water, and in most places chock full of native Brook Trout. The fish weren't big for the most part, but they were fun to catch. There had been reports of plenty of Green Drakes coming off a few of the feeder streams too.

It was well after two o'clock though and still no sign of the two. He was glad they'd paid their money up front. Increasingly, he was insisting on getting the money first. Too often, he haggled with clients who showed up late then insisted on paying only for the time spent on the water. He didn't much mind waiting though. The beer tasted fine and from his seat on the steps he could look through the branches of the rhododendrons and see parts of the Shad rushing by. He never grew tired of that.

It was quiet too, though it wouldn't stay that way for long. The lunch crowd was gone, and the only people left were a few of the hard-core drinkers, older locals who rarely left the barroom save to go home and sleep off yet another drunk. A lot of vehicles were still around the store, most of them owned by fishermen who had headed off to the stream. Soothsayer was out in the back, still tying flies for the invasion of fishermen due to arrive later for the Green Drake Hatch.

Soothsayer seemed to be moving more slowly these days. He rarely ventured out to the stream anymore and was spending more time upstairs in his room away from everyone. Tar had even mentioned something about overhearing Soothsayer talking on the telephone in the barroom with a lawyer.

"Now how do you know it was a lawyer?" Jack asked.

"'Because he mentioned something about a will," Tar said.

Soothsayer wasn't his old self. But Jack didn't want to believe the old guy was in failing health, or God forbid, dying. He knew the winter had been especially tough for Soothsayer, but then again, cold weather never did suit the old guy. He always had maintained that. "Keeps me inside and away from the stream," Soothsayer said.

Jack had just finished off his beer when he heard the car come off Highway 6 and make the turn into the narrow entrance road and rumble across the cattle guard over shallow Carpenter's Run that fed into the Shad. Jack watched the car slow to a stop in the parking lot. He didn't know much about cars, but if he wasn't mistaken, the well-polished and impressive model just twenty feet from where he sat was a Jaguar. This wasn't altogether out of the ordinary, given the number of Yuppies and older captains of industry who showed up to do fly-fishing anymore. But most of these hotshots had the good sense to arrive here in their four-wheelers, jeeps or other vehicles more conducive to mountain terrain rather than their "show" cars.

A man with refined features brought his tall trim frame smartly out of the vehicle. He had the chiseled prominent chin and the deep-set eyes of a man who'd spent some amount of time behind a desk fretting over important business matters, but a man too who'd perhaps properly and smartly enjoyed the fruits of his labors rather than surrendering to slovenly living. With a sudden tilt of his head, he sniffed the air about him. Having made a quick assessment of his surroundings, he abruptly swiveled about, and placing his hands on his hips, turned to face the Shad, the sound of the stream having no doubt reached his ears. But his eyes didn't linger long on the stream. Apparently, this wasn't a man given to long reflection about matters. There was about him, Jack noted, an uneasy sense of impatience. A city person, he figured.

When the man realized that he'd left his car door open, his hand suddenly shot out to slam it shut as if it had caused some transgression. In his other hand he held a roadmap. He slapped it against the sharp seam of the single leg of his slacks and faced the Roll Cast.

"Help ya?" Jack said.

If he even heard or noticed Jack sitting there, he didn't acknowledge it.

"Excuse me," he said, now facing Jack. "*This* is the Shad River?" He pointed behind him at the stream.

It was a statement more than a question and said with the sort of authoritative air of one who didn't relish being uncertain about matters.

Jack nodded.

"Splendid." He turned away and went to the car's passenger's side. "We are here Missy."

Jack caught sight of a blonde woman wearing sun glasses, her mouth upturned in a way that signaled anything but happiness.

"Howdy. My name's Jack McAllister. I believe I'll be your guide."

Jack got up from the steps and walked over to him, his hand extended. The man gave it a cool glance before suddenly taking it with a limp hand.

"Martin Ralston. It's a pleasure." He leaned down to the window. "Missy. Meet Jack McAllister. This is the gentleman who will be guiding us."

The woman frowned. It was not the scenario she had envisioned when they'd made plans for a weekend fishing trip last month: Lake George and a big airy ten-room cabin overlooking the water. Now *that* was her style. The little bungalow ten miles down the road was a dump, and now this. Some redneck in a scruffy beard. Good God. For two hundred bucks, she'd expected something a little more in the way of class. She sighed. This place, what was it called … The Roll Cast?

It certainly didn't look like much. Probably fatty hamburgers, cheap draft beer and local yokels who had all the charm of road kill. She liked the log cabin look though. A certain rustic element that might offer something, although she wasn't sure what. Still, it wasn't a place you wanted to linger about too long. Martin would probably delight in it all. Poor Martin. Always finding an adventure in things that were completely foreign to his own world. Perhaps that was precisely why he was so good at making money. This fly-fishing nonsense was a perfect example. Since taking a lesson in the sport a few years ago, it had been his intention to fly-fish every Godforsaken trout stream in America. He wanted nothing less than to have mounted in the den of his Greenwich townhouse a brown trout of "epic proportions," as he put it. That was Martin. Always caught up in myths and competitions of the renaissance man.

She had spent more than a few spring and summer weekends of the past few years in various backwater trout country. At first, it had been ... well ... fun. And the quick getaways to other states were refreshing. God knows, they both worked hard enough and needed these weekend jaunts. With a pilot's license and his own private plane, Martin could flee his Manhattan office on a Friday afternoon and be in Colorado for a late supper. Often, with a little proper planning they could find a decent French restaurant or even a show to attend in the evenings. That is, if they went to a stream within a couple hours driving distance of a town resembling a metropolis. But this place. Where in the hell was it? She doubted they could find a decent bottle of wine anywhere close by. She'd try to make the best of this situation. Plans called for her to even try her hand at some fly-fishing.

The barroom was pretty much to Missy's expectations. Everything from the fatty hamburgers, which she and Martin were both eager to devour—as they hadn't eaten since before leaving Connecticut early that morning—to the saw-dusted floor and the burly, bearded bartender, to the country music on the jukebox. Their fishing guide, Jack, seemed distant, if not aloof, somewhat rugged, a real working-class stiff who seemed a bit uncomfortable around them. While she and Martin ate their burgers and greasy fries, he remained at the bar with a beer before him, quietly talking with the fat barkeep. He was congenial enough, she supposed, though not in the eagerly friendly manner she'd experienced with guides elsewhere. She was kind of glad of that. Business was business after all, and even if a guide's means of earning a living was a bit unconventional, he needn't come off like a used-car salesman.

"You folks want to get out on the water pretty soon?" Jack asked from his barstool.

Martin was just chewing down the last bite of his burger. His head was turned, his eyes studying the trout mounted well above the jukebox. The fish had been taken by Jack the previous summer from Rock Run, a tiny feeder stream off the Shad. The day had been hot, the fishing slow on the Shad as it usually got in August, often the best time to hit cooler streams like Rock Run, where many trout retreated when the Shad's water temperatures became too warm. Jack had encountered a slow stretch of guiding at that time and used a day off to get in some fishing he so sorely missed.

As he explained it to the couple, the fish had grabbed a Number 14 Adams at the head of some riffles and tore off into a pool.

"It took me twenty minutes to bring that mother in," he said.

Martin's eyes quickly turned to Jack before focusing back on the trophy trout.

"That is a fine Brook Trout. I must say."

It was all Jack could do to keep from correcting the guy. *It's a Brown Trout you Goddamn idiot.*

Jack noted the guy smiling for the first time since the couple's arrival, even if the gleaming white teeth he showed were clenched. Jack knew the type. All business. The guy would not only want to know where were the biggest fish, he'd want to know precisely how to catch them too, as if there was any fool-proof, guaranteed way to latch onto the lunkers.

As for the woman, he wasn't sure what to make of her. She was attractive enough, as were many of these ladies who agreed to be dragged along on fishing trips with rich boyfriends. But there was a hardness about her, a kind of "I don't take shit" from you sort of attitude. It probably wasn't going to be one of his more enjoyable guiding trips.

"Tell me. Mr. McAllister. Where does one catch such a fine trophy fish?" He gave Jack a level-headed cool gaze.

Jack couldn't help but get into the spirit of things. "Well, sir, *one* catches such trophies just about anywhere around here."

Missy found herself stifling a laugh. The thing that had first attracted her to Martin other than his lofty ambitions were his Ivy League background and how he got right to the point. But she couldn't help but be amused by his stuffy, rigid schoolmaster persona, and his insistence on speaking in clear, grammatically correct sentences even when talking to rustics who likely didn't appreciate well-spoken English.

Jack stole a glance at Missy. For the first time, he thought: There might be more to this gal than meets the eye. Yeah. She was attractive enough in expensive neoprene waders from foot to chest that fit tightly over her slim body.

Her rod was a five-weight job, a graphite type of about eight feet. Just right for the Shad. And yet, she probably was less expensively outfitted than her boyfriend. Her rod probably cost about what old Martin had anted up for the net if his guess was right. He had to chuckle. It was the same old story. The boyfriends come out here with the bigger rods and the pricier outfits, expecting the equipment to enable them to catch the bigger fish.

"You might want to try some of these," Jack said, holding out some flies in the palm of his hand toward Martin and Missy. They had left the Roll Cast and were standing along the stream now. As usual, Jack was surveying the water for any fish rises, any sound of trout gulping the surface for flies.

Martin frowned as he surveyed the flies. "And those are7'

"March Browns. Number 12."

"Ah. Stenonemavicarium."

Jack never ceased to be amazed at the number of fly-fishermen anymore who could-spout off the Latin names for these flies, the same ones who often couldn't tell the difference between a common dry fly and a nymph.

"I saw a trout take one out near the rock just as we came down the path," Jack said, pointing toward an L-shaped boulder near the other side of the Shad.

"I see," Martin said, bringing a single hand to his brow as if shielding it from the sun and gazing out toward the rock.

Right off, Martin had problems casting. He was trying to get the line out near the rock at a point where the water came out of some riffles and fed into a long pool. Martin did have some sense of where the fish could be found. Jack had to give him that much. But his line and leader, rather than landing on the water like a feather, splattered upon the water in a heap with each cast.

Jack could see the trouble right off. At the release point, the guy was bringing the rod right out in front of him, almost vertical to the ground, rather than at a point just above his forehead. He was trying to force the line out on the water. The trout Jack had spotted earlier popped the surface about every half minute to grab a fly, and Martin was doing his damnedest to get his fly out there.

Jack wasn't surprised when Martin finally hooked himself in the hat. He was surprised to see him refrain from anger and not toss down his rod and spew profanities as he'd seen so many fishermen do in similar situations. Instead, Martin remained calm. He removed his hat and from his fishing vest, extracted a shiny pair of scissors which he used to snip the fly.

"Well. I must say," he said, breaking into a rare smile. *"That* has certainly never happened."

Just up the stream, Missy stood on a long flat rock with her rod, looking downstream toward her boyfriend and smiling. How amusing, she thought, that Martin could be so thorough and adept about his business affairs, but be so inept out here on a trout stream. How many times had he hooked himself? More times than she could count. He quite expected to be expert, or at least competent, in all facets of his life, and to see him fumble about here on a stream was rather pathetic. But then, when it came to anything requiring some degree of physical coordination, Martin was all thumbs.

Martin, to his credit, had the keen foresight to exclude himself from games of skill. Once, he'd recounted to her a painful childhood of being excluded from games, and his absolute refusal to take up golf despite their active membership in the country club was proof that Martin wasn't about to relive those boyhood humiliations. Martin endured the ribbing from fellow club members that his girlfriend could sometimes hold her own with some of the club's better male golfers. He was, after all, a competitor, who hated to take a back seat to anyone. It was an admirable trait, but at the same time exasperating.

This competitiveness had served him well in the business world, and he made no small bones about the fact that he'd made a pile of money in real estate while she was still under six figures as an editor of one of the country's more noted woman's magazines. Because she could be as competitive as him, there had been no small amount of friction between them.

Martin had his moods too. Often, he'd retreat into one of his damn funks. If a piece of property wasn't selling as he felt it should or one of his employees was screwing up, there was no talking to him. The man had his flaws, but then again who didn't?

She gazed downstream at Jack. He was standing on the bank with what appeared to be an amused look watching Martin fumble in his fly vest. She wondered what were his flaws.

Chapter 11

"Look at you. The luckiest son of a bitch on God's green earth," Tar said.

"Oh shit. Here we go again," Jack said.

Jack watched Tar wipe down the bar top for what seemed like the hundredth time. He didn't need this, especially on a hot August night, the hottest of a week-long stretch of blistering weather. The ceiling fans twirling above seemed to throw nothing but warm air around. "For the love of hell, would you give that rag a rest," Jack said. "You'll wipe a damn stain into the wood."

"You are numb nuts. You're the luckiest son of a bitch there is."

"Just give me a beer. Okay."

He could think of nothing more welcome than a cold beer. And for Tar to shut the hell up.

"Coming right up my lucky friend."

Tar put the beer down in front of Jack, propped his elbows on the bar. Placing his face about six inches from

Jack's, he grinned widely at his friend. "How's it feel to be in love old buddy?"

Jack felt his face flush. "Back off you goon," he said. He hoisted his beer as if to skull Tar before bringing it down to his lips.

"Now that hits the spot," Jack said.

"Like it? That's the last there is."

"What?"

"A bunch of hot and thirsty fishermen were in here earlier. Flashed a couple hundred bucks and bought out my supply."

"Naturally," Jack groaned.

"So how about it fella," Tar said. "Lucky in love?"

"Is that what you call it? In case you haven't heard, she stopped talking to me yesterday."

"Ain't love grand?" Tar began prancing about behind the bar and batting his eyes at Jack.

"Yeah. Just peachy."

"Oh-h-h-h-h ... Jack. I just l-u-u-u-v the way you are ... "

Tar reached down to pinch his cheek. Jack fought a grin and looked around the barroom. "Careful. Someone might come down off the mountain and whisk you away."

"Oh-h-h-h-h ... whisk me away ... whisk me away ... dear Jack." Tar continued prancing about, twirling the beer rag round and round.

"God you're a silly shit," Jack said.

Tar stopped prancing. All at once, he gave Jack an appraising look.

"C'mon Jack. Admit it. You're lucky."

"Yeah. Right."

"Cut the shit. The best-looking gal in these parts and you're getting it. I'd say that's worth the drawbacks."

"You don't know the half of it."

Jack wondered if *he* knew the half of it. What a strange summer it had been. One night, he'd been crawling into bed with Missy, the next thing he knew, she had thrown away a job in New York, tossed aside Martin, moved into the fishing cabin of a retired and ailing Williamsburg physician who had agreed to lease it to her, and practically assumed control of his guide business. Funny thing was, he had allowed it all to happen. Jack McAllister, who did no man's bidding but his own, who'd done his damnedest to live life on his own terms, had indeed fallen in love, hopelessly and ridiculously in love with Missy of New York, New York. At least, he guessed that's what he could call it. God knows, they often fought like two cats in a cage, and over the stupidest stuff, only to make up and start in again days later.

The latest flare-up had begun over Jack's utter refusal to bring along Chardonnay wine, cheese and crackers for a group of Yuppies he was about to guide. The late summer Slate Drake hatch had been heating up pretty good in recent days, and this group, three college professors, had driven down from Cornell University to catch it.

"They specifically requested the Chardonnay," Missy said, all but tossing the wine bottle into the cooler. The cooler was a beat-up thing, and Jack had been using it for years to pack away beer and soda, but never wine, for God sakes. Naturally, she'd be on his ass half the summer about replacing the thing with something with a bit more style. Just as she was forever on him about getting rid of his patched-up neoprene waders, giving up the tattered ball cap he'd been wearing out on the stream since the Reagan Administration and, the worst of all, saying so long to the pickup truck.

"When is it going to occur to you Jack that you're a businessman. Appearances count."

Appearances count. He'd been hearing that from her too. It had become a refrain, a litany she insisted on driving into his head.

One morning, he'd woken up to find a picture torn from one of his fly-fishing magazines plastered on the wall of his living room. The photograph, oh-so-typical of those publications, displayed a trim handsome fella casting his line along a gorgeous stretch of some unnamed stream. Of course, the guy was well-outfitted in the most expensive fly-fishing attire—a point Missy had made careful note of. With a pen, she had scribbled these arrows on the photo, the arrows pointing to the pricey clean-looking vest, the top-of-the-line waders, the fashionable wide-brimmed hat, the net dangling from his hip, its polished gleaming handle glistening in the sun. Under the photograph, she'd scrawled: Appearances count!

Naturally.

Not that he hadn't heeded any of her "suggestions." Take her advertising.

Except for two or three of the more noted fly-fishing publications, Jack had pretty much ignored using magazines to advertise. He'd always felt the prices were exorbitant, and word of mouth had always brought him clients. It's how he had done business for years. Missy had him placing ads for his guiding services in no less than a dozen magazines, including some of the publications targeted to other outdoor sports. Jack had resisted at first, but starting at the end of July when his answering machine became flooded with guiding requests, even he had to admit that her suggestions were a sound investment.

Her contacts in the magazine world had brought more business. A travel writer from a Philly newspaper and former co-worker of Missy's had fished the Shad one weekend and done a nice write-up that had brought him more clients than he really needed. She had convinced another ex-colleague of hers, now an editor for a trendy East Coast magazine, to send a writer to the Green Valley to do an article. Jack was still bracing himself for the crush of fishermen following that piece's publication.

Summer was usually slow, what with the water often getting a bit warm and the Green Drake Hatch long over. But this year, thanks to Missy, business had picked up in these slower months. Hell, he'd even given up his annual Montana trip in August. Every year, he went out there with the local Trout Unlimited group for a week or so of fishing. Usually, there were no more than one or two fishermen interested in his guiding service at that time of year, and he could count on getting Tar to take care of that. Tar didn't know shit about fly-fishing; he was a bait caster, for God sakes, but he knew the Shad about as well as anyone. Tar could always give him a hand when he needed it.

Missy, of course, tried to put an end to it.

"The man's far too crude," she said. "He'll scare away more business than anything."

"I'll need him, probably more than ever," Jack insisted.

Jack had stood fast on this, and for three days the two had stopped talking.

This was right around the Fourth of July when the fishing normally slowed down on The Shad. She left early the next morning with word that she was driving into Williamsburg "for some shopping." He had found this a little strange, considering that during the short month or so of her living in the Green Valley, she'd gone to great lengths to avoid Williamsburg at all costs, referring to it as "a one-horse town with absolutely no cultural refinements."

When she returned late that afternoon, Jack was sitting on the front steps of his cabin working a leg into his patched-up waders.

"Wearing those again I see," she said. She was out of the car, staring at him behind her sunglasses. "Do you suppose you could help me with some of these things."

Jack was horrified to see the boxes were holding a computer, a fax machine and printer and a telephone.

"Oh no," he said. "They're not going in here."

"No worries," she said with a grin. "They're going to my place."

Which is exactly where they went. And just like that, Jack realized he now had a business office about a half mile down the road.

Not that he completely minded. But it often stymied him why Missy had taken such an interest in his business. Or an interest in him for that matter. How in the hell had they become a couple? Their first night together that evening in late May at the height of the Green Drake Hatch had been a disaster in his mind—at least sexually. On the drive down to Williamsburg she'd made up her mind to end her relationship with Martin. No explanation, no teary regrets. No. He hadn't read anything into that.

At the hospital, they'd gone their separate ways— she to see Martin recovering from a broken arm after taking a nasty spill in the Shad and him to visit Soothsayer. The old man had been having dizzy spells and finally, at the behest of Jack and Tar, agreed to have himself checked into the hospital. Soothsayer's stay at the hospital was no more than a day, and Jack was relieved to know that his old buddy would be okay.

As for Missy, he figured, with a tinge of regret, he'd never see her again. But then again, that's the way it always was with the women in his life. To his surprise, she'd turned up more than a week later on that June day outside his cabin behind the wheel of a Volvo. And well ... he'd been damn happy about it. By then the Green Drake Hatch had ended and he was settling in for another slow summer.

Yeah, Missy had come into his life all right, and he was still trying to make sense of it.

"Sooth thinks it's a good thing. That's for damn sure," Tar said.

"You mean me and Missy?" Jack rolled his eyes. "I know. Believe me I know."

Tar's expression turned grave. "You seen him lately? He's been looking better."

Jack nodded. He *had* been looking better.

"I was a little worried when he had that spell outside here that one night, but yeah, since getting out of the hospital he's been his old self."

"And how are you doing? The leg still bothering you?"

Jack ran his hand across his knee cap. A fall in the stream a week earlier had laid him up for a couple of days. It had gotten better, but he was surprised to find it still swollen and with him still limping.

"I think it might be getting better," Jack said.

The telephone in the bar rang.

"It's your wife...er ... girlfriend," Tar grinned, holding the phone.

It was Missy. She was alone back at his place. Could he come right away? There was something important she wanted to discuss with him.

"Guess I'll hit the road," Jack said as he returned to his seat.

Tar shook his head. "Don't tell me it ain't love."

Jack drank down the rest of his beer. With a thud, he brought it down on the bar.

"Tar. You're okay. I don't care what anyone says."

"Yeah. You can wear my underwear too."

"So long Tar. And may all your dreams be wet ones."

Jack's was the only cabin along the five-minute walk from the Roll Cast. A thick forest of pines and maples all but swallowed the cabin from view. At night, by the time he was halfway home, he could always see the light he kept on in the living room. But not this time. It was not until he was almost to the cabin that he saw there was some light after all.

Inside, he found a pair of candles flickering on the coffee table, and a few others as well at the kitchen table and on the windowsills of the living room. Jack heard the softest of mood music coming from the bedroom.

"Hello," a husky voice called to him. It was Missy.

"What the hell's going on here. A seance?"

It was kind of spooky. The candles on the coffee table threw shadows and weird formations about the walls and ceiling of his cabin. For a fleeting instant he wondered if possibly Missy was a member of some strange religious cult she hadn't told him about. She was a woman full of surprises.

"Come in here," she said.

Flames from still other candles flickered atop his dresser. Missy was naked, sitting on the edge of his bed staring at him in the near darkness, a mysterious smile playing about her lips.

"I thought you might enjoy some company tonight," she said.

"Might be nice," he said, his own words sounding strange to him.

He could see her staring at him through the darkness.

Jack began moving about the room, aware of Missy smiling, watching him. He turned on the box fan sitting in the corner next to his dresser. He went to the room's single window and peered out through the blinds into the darkness. Resting above the pines was a quarter moon bathed by the night haze. He moved over to the bed. It squeaked under his weight. He was vaguely aware of the fan blowing balmy air on him. He sat there, feeling sticky and uncomfortable in his waders. The next thing he knew, she had moved right up beside him to slip a hand down the back of his shirt. The palm of her hand began slowly massaging the small of his back. "Look, let's just do it," she said softly.

The massaging felt good as did her tongue running down his spine. Maybe it would happen this time. Jack lowered himself face-down on the bed and let her go to work on him. She undressed him and proceeded to rub, massage and perform teasing, titillating maneuvers that should have driven him at least half crazy. But Jack felt only the faintest of stirrings.

When it was all too apparent that once again, there would be no real lovemaking, Missy stretched her naked body out beside Jack on the bed, emitting a long sigh.

"Can a girl get a smoke around here?" she asked.

"Top drawer of the dresser," he said.

She turned to him. "I was kidding. I didn't think you smoked."

"I don't. They're for my bedroom companions."

She lightly backhanded him on the shoulder and got up from the bed. He tried to lose himself in the whirring noise of the fan. He heard her footsteps move back and forth across the room and the noise of her scratching a match to light up one of the cigarettes. She fell back onto the bed. For the longest time, they didn't talk.

"I suppose it's silly to think it's me," Missy finally said.

Jack said nothing.

"Perhaps, we should consider some other measures. I know a wonderful therapist in Manhattan."

"Some shrink to charge me five hundred bucks an hour, just so I can tell him I masturbated with *Playboy* when I was thirteen years old. Forget it."

"Five hundred is hardly the going rate. But at any cost, it's well worth it, I can assure you."

"Personal experience Missy?"

"Please. You're hardly in position to be examining another's sex life."

Jack knew only too well that was true. "Maybe I need to try something kinky. How about toe sex?"

Missy seemed to ignore this.

"I suppose I could drop hints at the lodge about your inability to perform in bed. Why, just imagine the shock from your fan base. Rough and tumble, two-fisted Jack McAllister, the macho fishing guide who can't get it up."

"You do that, and they'll be a line of men from your place back to the lodge hoping to take a shot at you."

"Well ..." Missy said, taking a long drag from the cigarette and watching the smoke quickly dissipate from the blowing fan into the darkness of the room. "I've always envied harem girls."

This had been the way it had gone most of the summer. The foreplay, that never seemed to thoroughly arouse Jack, the frustration of no intercourse. And all summer, they'd joked and laughed about it all. Missy had been a pretty good sport about it too. Still, the drift of these conversations often made him uncomfortable. How long was she going to wait for him to perform?

"You start screwing other guys, and I just might be able to get it up," Jack said quite seriously.

"Don't worry dear," Missy said, softly rubbing his shoulders. 'We'll work it out."

"I meant to tell you," she said. "That friend of yours ... that man who refers to himself as a lawyer stopped by the office today."

Jack was only too happy to have the subject switch from sex to another topic.

"Adamly?"

"That's the person. He has a way of leering, I must say."

"Leering?"

"I think he was mentally undressing me. I leered right back. I'm not sure what sort of effect it had on him, however. He doesn't strike me as a man easy to embarrass."

"That's just what I need. For you to go to bed with some lawyer and then have me knock him on his ass."

"I think he's sleazy and disgusting. But I could be wrong."

"You don't know the half of it."

Missy sat up and looked intently at Jack. "Is he still trying to convince you to put up money for that hunting lodge?"

"Yeah. How do you know about that?"

"You told me."

"I did? I don't think so."

"Whatever. It might be something to consider. Real estate is nothing to turn one's nose up at."

"Hey. I thought you said he was a sleaze."

"Even a sleaze can turn out to have wonderful business acumen."

Jack watched Missy take a deep, luxurious drag on the cigarette.

"He thinks he can rent rooms out of that place to fishermen and hunters and hikers. Or even something else," Jack said. "I've told him up front I don't want anything in the way of development there. Especially, if it's going to hurt the fishing."

"I see. What's on your agenda tomorrow?" she asked.

"Sooth and me are heading up to Arnie Fausnaught's in the morning."

"Are you referring to the farmer who heads up that conservation group? What's it called?"

"Trout Unlimited. The local chapter. Arnie's keeps a tab on things around here. Cleaning up the stream and such. We get together with him every now and then just to get updated."

"I see," she said.

Chapter 12

All his life, Soothsayer had been a sound sleeper, untroubled by insomnia or bad dreams. An early riser, he was usually in bed by ten thirty and up by five the following morning. This was his sleeping pattern all his adult life, and it was rarely interrupted, despite living directly above the barroom, when revelry and noise from below would have surely distracted others.

As usual, he'd gone to bed early. After bidding goodnight to Jack and Tar down in the barroom around nine thirty, he'd disappeared into the back where he'd climbed the stairs to his single room. Upstairs, the room was stifling from the summer heat, and he turned the air conditioner on high to cool things down.

A few summers previously, when the Green Spring Valley had been hit by a horrible drought, Soothsayer had allowed Tar to lend him the secondhand one that he'd repaired. Soothsayer had never seen the need for air conditioning, having lived without it all his life. The nights usually brought cool air filtering in from the mountains anyway, but it had been a particularly hot and unbearable summer, even for him. And so, the air conditioner had remained, even if he rarely ran the thing, save for times like this when the day's heat and humidity hung in the air.

He usually went right to sleep, but as his head hit the pillow this night, he thought about how things had taken a turn for the good in recent months. His health had rebounded, and activity had settled down a bit with the end of the Green Drake Hatch in June. Summer had always been a time to kick back, although he was starting to see that those lazy summers of the past were slipping away with each year. Things were changing. That was clear. More fishermen were discovering the Shad, but so far, the invasion wasn't too bad, save for the spring months, and especially that two-week period during the Green Drake Hatch. And he and Jack and some of the other concerned folks in Trout Unlimited had taken some measures to ensure the fishing didn't get ruined by the onslaught.

The extension of the Shad's catch and release area for another few miles kept the bait fishermen away—at least in that part of the stream—and helped to boost the Shad's supply of reproducing Brown and Brook Trout. And now, if they could convince the state fish agency to stop stocking the stream, the wild and native trout population would continue to flourish. Still, you could only do so much. Long ago, he had come to accept the fact that change was inevitable.

Tranquil thoughts flooded his brain as he fell off into a deep sleep. But around midnight, he woke up with a start. Something was wrong. Exactly what, he didn't know. He quickly got into some clothes and headed to the barroom. Occasionally, but not often, disturbances of one kind or another were known to occur downstairs.

Tar, who was finishing up closing the barroom, assured him all was fine. He did say the beer had run out and they'd need to get on the phone in the morning to have the distributor make an emergency run.

"You go on back to bed old man. I'm going to lock up."

Which Sooth did. But sleep didn't come. Something continued to gnaw at him. His powers of accurate prognostication usually portended positive events, and when these rare foreboding thoughts creeped into his mind, he couldn't ignore them. Rarely, if ever, could he pin down the calamitous event or tragedy sure to follow. He could be almost certain that something unwelcome, something unwanted was about to occur, that is, if it hadn't already happened. And there wasn't a damn thing he could do about it.

The next morning, he met Jack as planned outside the Roll Cast. Fay was busy in the kitchen cooking up eggs and bacon for the few locals and one or two fishermen who already had stopped by for an early breakfast. Soothsayer rarely drank coffee, but he was tired from little sleep and had Fay bring him a cup at the bar.

Fay gave him an appraising look as she set the coffee before him. "Tar said you was up at midnight. That ain't like ya. Ya okay?"

In fact, he felt drained. All night long, he'd tossed and turned in the bed wrestling with the dark feeling that had dominated his thoughts. He looked at the hard-worn round face of Fay. Blunt and tough-spoken with most everyone else around the bar, she was always sweet with Soothsayer, inquiring about his health and sharing things with him from her life.

Fay's was not an easy life, what with raising four kids and a husband working as a bartender with her at the Roll Cast. He was glad to have given her and Tar some employment when they'd been down. The fact that they'd both stayed on longer than originally planned was fine with him. They were his kind of people—simple, hardworking mountain folks like him and Jack.

"Excuse me Fay, but I think I'll take this coffee with me out on the porch."

Outside, it was an overcast morning, with the hint of rain in the air. For two weeks, the Green Valley had baked from the late-summer heat. The Shad had lost much of its hard flow and was sorely in need of a good dose of rain. And now, looking over the tops of the pine trees where he could see gray clouds blanketed by the haze, it appeared the stranglehold of the harsh blistering weather was about to be loosened. The warm air stirred with a gentle breeze. Soothsayer heard gentle rumblings of thunder from off in the distance.

The trip to Arnie's farm was just upstream from The Flats, about a twenty-minute drive, most of it along a twisting, mountainous dirt road off Highway 6. Having only caught bits and pieces of sleep after waking up the previous night, Soothsayer dozed in the front seat of Jack's pickup truck as it bumped along the dirt road that wound its way through the forested hills of the Green Valley.

Emerging from the woods, the road dipped sharply downward before flattening out into a meadow area. Jersey cows grazed in the field behind a fence. Up ahead loomed a red barn and a cone-shaped silo. And farther back, the weathered white house Arnie called home.

Several chickens scampered away as Jack drove up the dirt road that ended in the grassless front lawn of Arnie's farmhouse. Jack hit the horn and seconds later the plump and baldheaded figure of Arnie emerged from a nearby storage shed. A man of few words, he nodded at them both and walked over to Jack sitting behind the wheel of the pickup.

"How's it going there Arnie," Jack said. 'Ya gettin' any?"

Arnie flushed red. He was a lifelong bachelor who had remained alone on the family farm after his parents had died. Every morning, he rose at four o'clock and milked each one of the fifty-two cows on his farm. He also shoveled the manure, fixed the equipment and did most everything else that needed done around the farm.

"Don't have time for that," he said simply, his thumbs twitching the suspenders of his bib overalls.

"Come on Arnie," Jack said. "Sooth here said he saw you leaving the bar one night with one of the Tracy twins."

The Tracy twins were neighbors of Arnie's, two rather large middle-aged spinsters who lived together in the same big stone farmhouse in which they'd grown up.

"Go on Jack. You know better than that."

"I don't know there Arnie. You better grab one of them twins while the gettin' is good."

"Go on," Arnie said, fighting an embarrassed grin.

"Looks like rain coming' up in that direction," Soothsayer said, anxious to move the topic away from sex.

"Yep. Look there," Arnie said, pointing a stubby finger toward the western sky.

An ominous black cloud loomed above the line of trees which separated the one end of the meadow from the Shad.

"How about that contribution Arnie?" Jack asked. "Are you going to be able to donate this time around?"

Arnie was not only president of Green Valley Trout Unlimited, he was the group's most generous donor. The money that he gave ultimately went toward helping The Shad. In various parts of the stream, especially here near Arnie's farm just below its origin, siltation problems had been known to interrupt its steady flow. Some pools in various parts of the stream had become almost stagnant, at times jeopardizing if not killing off some of the wild trout population. Arnie's land bordered both sides of the Shad, and he'd been known to put up the necessary funds and made sure that proper streambank restoration had been done.

"Ah fellas. I don't know if I can swing it this time."

Soothsayer looked from Arnie to Jack then back at Arnie.

"What's wrong Arnie? Are you having a tough year farming?"

Arnie ran the back of his hand across the leathery, sun-scorched skin of his forehead. "That's part of it fellas. Plus ..."

"What is it?" Jack asked.

Arnie bowed his head and ran a single hand repeatedly over his bald pate. He kicked at the dirt. He raised his head. "I had to sell off some land this summer just to make ends meet."

"I don't get it Arnie," Jack said.

"Maybe you fellas better follow me."

The three of them cut across the meadow toward the line of trees. The Shad was about a five-minute walk and the wind just beginning to sweep through the valley carried the scent of the impending storm.

Soothsayer realized he hadn't been here in years. Beyond the line of trees, he could see the ridge. As a young man he'd cut across this very field and climbed to the very top of that hill. There had been a very special lady he'd courted in those days, the only true love in his long life, and one Sunday afternoon, he'd brought her to the summit. The two of them had brought a picnic lunch that sunny May afternoon, spreading a blanket on the soft carpet of grass beneath the branches of a great maple tree just a short cast from the Shad, where it began as little more than a trickle before beginning its long descent down the mountain. And there, Soothsayer had made love to the woman, for the first and as it turned out, the last time.

The woman, her name was Jess, died tragically in an automobile accident the very next day. Soothsayer had mourned over her death and was convinced that he would never know another woman like Jess. For the rest of his life, he never again bothered with another woman. And he never again made love to one.

At a small clearing at the top of the bank along the stream, a pair of large crows were chewing on the carcass of a deer. They paused from feasting on the deer at the approach of the three men before flying off with cackling noises. At the clearing, the trio stood gazing down at the water.

"Water sure is brown up here," Jack said.

"Sure is," Soothsayer added. "That don't seem right to me."

"Over there," Arnie pointed.

Soothsayer and Jack counted four dead trout belly-up in a pool on the stream's far side.

"Shit," Jack said.

"I hate to tell you fellas this," Arnie said sadly. "But there's more."

Rain began to fall lightly as Arnie led them upstream along a path following the Shad. The path was overrun by knee-high ferns, raspberry bushes and occasional poison ivy, and Arnie used a stick to knock away the growth. As they walked, Soothsayer and Jack saw more trout drifting on their backs downstream.

"This is where it's the worst," Arnie said.

Arnie didn't have to point this time. The three of them gazed at the dozens of trout floating belly-up in the stagnant water of a large pool. A great heap of tree branches had gathered in a slow eddy at its tail end. Here, and in other spots along the stream, trout were floating lifelessly in the nearly still water.

"Jesus Christ," Jack said.

"Lordy. Lordy," Soothsayer said.

Jack limped down to the stream's edge. He bent over and stuck a single hand in the water. The water felt warm but no warmer than it had felt a few days earlier when he had taken a seventy-three-degree reading of the stream. The highest temperature he'd ever recorded for the stream was 76 degrees back in the summer of '88 when only a few trout had turned up dead.

Arnie turned away from the scene and ran a hand repeatedly over his bald pate. "It's my fault doggone it. I shoulda seen it comin'."

"What are you talking about Arnie?" Jack said.

"Them boys tricked me I'm tellin' ya," Arnie said, barely able to keep his voice from cracking. "I'm tellin' ya. They tricked me."

It began to rain harder. Big drops pelted the stream.

Soothsayer placed a hand on Arnie's shoulder. "Who tricked you Arnie?" he said gently.

"Oh, damn it all. It was that there lawyer friend of yours Jack."

Jack trudged up the bank, dragging his bad leg behind him. "You mean Adamly?"

"That's the fella. He and another fella said they was looking to get an easement. Seemed like nice enough men. Something about needing to come on my land to make stream improvements. Then they said never mind about the easement. They offered money to just buy a piece of my land … and well ..."

"When was this Arnie?" Jack said.

"A few months ago, I guess. I screwed up. Didn't I?"

"Oh my. Oh no," Soothsayer said.

Jack peered out at the stream at a few of the dead trout floating belly-up in the water.

"Let me get this straight," he said. "They bought some of your land?"

"Yep," Arnie said, staring forlornly at the ground.

"Okay," Jack said. "But that doesn't explain ..."

"I think it does son," Soothsayer said, nodding upstream.

"Oh God," Jack said.

On the opposite side of the Shad, far upstream, a huge swath of trees had been cut away nearly as far as he could see. Stumps dotted the bank and ran halfway up a ridge.

"Clearcutting. *Damn*," Jack said.

The three of them stood along the bank, just staring at the damage to the terrain.

"I feel downright awful. Just downright awful," Arnie said. He began to sob.

Jack wanted to say something. But what really was there to say? You sure as hell couldn't quickly replace a bunch of trees. Thank God, this area of the Shad rarely if ever was fished. He just hoped like hell it didn't affect the trout population farther downstream.

"Well ... that's that," he said. "I suppose we should get back. What do you say Sooth? Sooth? Oh shit ..."

The old man was on the ground, lying face-up with a dazed expression.

Chapter 13

Jack sat vigil at Soothsayer's bedside that night at the hospital in Williamsburg. The good news was that Soothsayer had not suffered a stroke or heart attack or any other kind of serious health problem.

"Exhaustion," I'd say," reported the young doctor who'd first seen Soothsayer in the emergency room.

Soothsayer appeared pale and altogether worn-out as he remained in bed, fading in and out of sleep. It seemed strange to Jack to see his old buddy in a hospital bed, a man who had always exuded the outdoors and healthy living.

Jack looked at the complex machines surrounding his bed. The doctor and the one nurse who occasionally appeared in the room told him they were checking his heart rate "just to be sure."

The volume of the single television across the room was off but the flickering images showed a police show. A chase scene was unfolding with a pair of cops in pursuit of a dark-hooded figure through city streets.

Soothsayer was on his back, looking weary and older than ever, his tired eyes staring at the television. "I hope they catch him," he said.

Jack looked from Soothsayer to the TV screen. The two cops were doing their best to keep up with the agile culprit, who had just leaped from one rooftop to another. He looked back to Soothsayer. "I didn't know you were really watching this."

Soothsayer slowly brought up a single hand and waved it dismissively at the TV. "I'm talking about that lawyer fella."

"You mean Adamly?"

Soothsayer nodded. "That's him."

Jack studied Soothsayer. As much as the whole situation angered him … all those dead trout in the Shad River, and what it would mean for fishing there, not to mention his business, he knew this was probably killing Soothsayer. The Shad River and the whole beautiful Green Valley had been the old man's entire life.

"The thing is," Jack said. "I don't know if he's done anything illegal. I mean … it's private property. "The son-of-a-bitch."

"That river dies …." Soothsayer began to say.

"And we're all screwed," Jack said.

"That river dies and …"

"And … what?"

"And … and I die," Soothsayer said.

He closed his eyes tightly.

Oh no, Jack thought. The old man *was* going to die.

He heard Soothsayer emit a low guttural moan and with his eyes still shut, turn on to his side. "I just want to sleep," he said in a low whisper. "Sleep … forever."

Jack said nothing. He studied Soothsayer for any signs of him slipping into death. Jesus … death. It was not something he wanted to think about. But there it was.

"You aren't really going to die? Are you?"

It was a stab at humor, a way of lightening the moment.

"Sooth. You hear me?"

The corners of Soothsayer's mouth upturned in a grin.

"The great Green Drake Hatch," he said, his eyes remaining closed, the smile appearing wider now.

Jack wasn't sure if the old man was dreaming or talking to him directly.

"Yeah. The great Green Drake Hatch," Jack said. "It's been something. Huh?"

Soothsayer slowly opened one eye, then the other. He had that dreamy, far-off look of a man who's perhaps had a vision, a remarkable insight into something beautiful, perhaps unexplainable to mere mortals.

"We did our part kid," he said. "We did our part."

The eyes went shut, and Soothsayer's head seemed to bury deep into the pillow. And at that moment, Jack knew his old buddy was gone.

It was raining when Jack left the hospital, lightly at first, but then heavily, like a relentless attack on the earth as he drove north back home to his cabin. Driving the narrow two-lane road along the Shad River, he caught glimpses of the stream and some of the spots where he had enjoyed fishing for so many years.

Somehow, he knew things had changed forever. Soothsayer's death. It would take him a long time to come to grips with that. Already, he missed his old buddy. But he had this strong, unshakeable feeling that his death meant the end of other things too.

He went first to the Roll Cast to give the news to Tar that Soothsayer was dead. But after turning off the highway and into the dirt parking lot of the bar-restaurant where he'd spent so much time over the years to relax with a beer or sandwich after a long day on the stream, he could tell something was amiss. It was just nine o'clock, but the Roll Cast was dark and empty looking.

On the front door was a sign: "Closed till further notice."

Why was the place closed? And where was Tar? Or Fay? There was no way they could have already known about Soothsayer's death.

Jack trudged through the rain back to his pickup truck. From behind the wheel of his truck, he could look out the rain-soaked windshield and just make out the blurry images of the Shad River. If the rain kept up like this, the stream would be swollen and running the color of chocolate by tomorrow.

He was surprised to see the light from the front window of his cabin when he pulled up in his pickup. A figure moved past the window just as he turned off the engine. He knew it had to be Missy. She was the only one other than him with a key to the place. But why was she here?

He was just to the front porch when the front door burst open and she was in his arms. She pressed up against him hard, clinging almost desperately to him. "Oh God. I didn't know. I didn't know." She was sobbing.

"It's all right. It's all right," Jack said. He found himself stroking her long hair as she pressed even harder into his body.

And then, it was all he could do to fight the tears. They clung to each other as they retreated into the cabin and fell together onto the couch. He didn't remember the last time he'd cried. Maybe when he'd had his first glimpse of the Madison River out in Idaho and seen all those rings on the water–trout rising for mayflies on that fabled western stream, a dream come true for a fly fisherman.

Tough guy Jack. Hell, he never cried. But maybe now it was okay—to have a good cry. His best friend was gone. Hell yeah, it was okay to let the tears flow. From outside he could hear the rain pounding, rattling the tin roof of his front porch. Missy had her face snuggled into his chest.

"I didn't know. I didn't know," she sobbed.

"Yeah. He died peacefully. In his sleep."

Jack felt Missy stiffen in his arms. "He was a good man, my best friend, my mentor, the dad you might say I never had." He really was tearing up now.

"The old man? He died?" she said.

"I thought you knew?"

Missy untangled herself from Jack. Now what? she thought. Should she tell him? How could she explain to him that it had been Martin, her ex-boyfriend, who had done the deal. Put up a lot of the money to buy that land with some locals under the recently formed Green Valley Landowners Association. She'd signed off on the deal too, but pretty much in name only. Okay. She wanted to make a little money too. Still, she'd had no idea they were looking to build a golf course and a resort and despoil a lot of land to do it.

"Okay. What is it Missy?"

And so, she told him.

He knew he should have seen it coming. Missy loved money, nice things, the so-called good life. Money, he'd come to realize during their brief and strange courtship, had a strange effect on Missy. Each morning, she headed down to Junction Corners, the store about fifteen miles down the road and the only place within miles that sold the *Wall Street Journal*.

Over a cup of coffee, she'd sit, poring over the financial pages. She claimed to know little about finances, although she conceded to have picked up a bit from Martin. Whenever she and Jack were out and around, driving about the mountains, it seemed her eye was forever trained about the landscape for commercial possibilities. She was forever talking about locating a bed & breakfast somewhere in the area. That would have been fine. There was not one to be found in the Green Valley, a fact Missy was not remiss about mentioning on more than one occasion. But a golf course and resort hotel? That was something else entirely.

Missy was sitting on the edge of the couch, her head buried in her arms, sobbing silently.

Jack wanted her out of his cabin.

"Those tears. Are they real?" he asked.

Slowly, she raised her head and stared at him through tear-streaked eyes.

"What do you think?" she said.

"I don't know. You tell me."

It was all in the next day's edition of the newspaper, several stories screaming on the front page written by Ron Noble. Jack sat on a bar stool of the Roll Cast reading through the whole sorry sordid mess as the rain continued to pound down outside.

The names of all the people involved with the Green Valley Landowners Association were finally revealed for all to see. Yeah. Missy was listed, along with her ex-boyfriend, Martin. And other names he recognized too. There were a half-dozen of them, owners of cabins along the Shad in the area below and above The Flats. He only had a nodding acquaintance with most of these people, some of whom only showed up a few weekends a year to fish or hunt.

The main story chronicled it all. Judge Garrity made it clear it was time for more people to enjoy "God's wonderful landscape here in the Green Valley." There was room, he said, for anglers, hunters *and* golfers, *maybe even skiers.*

Skiers? Jesus, Jack thought. He read on through all the pages. Arnie Fausnaught, God bless him, had been interviewed. He said it was "a shame, a darn shame" what might happen to the Green Valley. "We don't need more people up there. It's perfect the way it is, something like heaven." He was, he said, saddened more than angry.

And Adamly. Sure, he was mentioned in one of the articles too. He was the attorney alright for the Green Valley Landowners Association, but he had offered no comment.

"It's a fuckin' shame," Tar said, standing on the other side of the bar as Jack finished reading the articles. "Damn Adamly. He's making this all happen. He oughta be taken out and shot."

"Ah hell, this place needs more people. Maybe this golf course or ski resort or whatever the hell they're thinking about putting up there will bring some jobs, some progress here."

Jack looked down at end of the bar where an old man sat slumped before a mug of beer. His face was dry and weathered like someone who'd done a lot of outside work. With his faded blue jeans, tattered plaid shirt and ball cap that nearly hid his eyes from view, he had to be someone from around these parts, and yet, Jack couldn't place him.

"No fella," Tar said, in an annoyed tone. "That's the last thing we need."

"It's called the future my friend," the man said, his eyes peering at Tar from beneath the cap.

"You're an asshole," Tar said.

"My friend. You're blind to reality."

Tar brought a single heavy fist down on the bar. His eyes were wide and angry. "Get out," he said.

The man remained unfazed. For a few moments, he stared at his beer, before reaching into his pocket and tossing a few dollars on the bar. With some effort, he stood up, smiled at Tar and then at Jack, before exiting the Roll Cast and heading out into the rain.

"Who was that guy?" Tar said.

Jack shrugged. "Someone from the dark side."

Chapter 14

That night, after the daylong rain had slowed down to just sprinkles, Jack got into his waders, put on his fishing vest, and took out his best bamboo fly rod. It was his favorite rod, but one he rarely used. He had bought it for several hundred dollars—a steal really—from a man out West during one of his summer fishing trips.

It was near dusk when he came off the porch of his cabin. He looked back at home, his place, his retreat, his refuge for all these years. How do you say good-bye to a home? He didn't have a clue. He turned and trudged through the sloppy terrain toward the Roll Cast. The Shad, with its swollen high waters from all the rain, roared nearby. It was no evening to be fishing its waters. But as far as Jack was concerned, it was the perfect time to fish the stream.

The two figures were standing on the porch of the Roll Cast as he emerged from the path along the stream.

"Hey buddy," Tar yelled to him. "Got something to tell ya. It's great."

"Mr. McAllister. I wanted to talk to you."

He could see the other figure was Ron Noble, the reporter.

Jack didn't want to talk to either of them, nor anyone else. He had this thing he had to do. And now Tar and Noble were sloshing across the mud and rain-soaked dirt parking lot toward him. "Just talked to Arnie," Tar said in an excited tone. "His Trout Unlimited group. They wanna fight this. They got some funds and some political might to stop this fuckin' progress from happening."

"Mr. McAllister. There's more," Noble said. "That land up there in The Flats. You probably know it wasn't zoned for commercial purposes, but now, interesting enough, it is. I have several people on record that claim there might have been a pay-off."

Jack saw the excitement in the young man's eyes. Once, he'd been young and felt that way about things, like fishing and living here in the Green Valley.

"I'm putting together more stories. This isn't over."

Jack looked from the reporter to Tar. What could he tell them? It was too late? It was over? That everything here, this whole wonderful Green Valley and the Shad and the trout in it and that Green Drake Hatch had all been an illusion?

"What the hell ya doin' anyway?" Tar said, looking Jack up and down now with a quizzical expression. "You ain't goin' fishing tonight. Hell, the stream's too damn high for that."

Jack reached out to give Tar a manly pat on his shoulder. "It's the best time to be fishing Tar."

He turned and left them both standing in the parking lot.

A few minutes later, he was on the edge of the swollen waters at The Bend, gazing through the misty dusk at the stream. It was the place to do it, where he and Soothsayer had come that evening years earlier to discover the return of the Great Green Drake Hatch.

The stream was well over its banks, the brown water rushing past. Branches and twigs and leaves moved by like a slow parade in the stream before him. For a few moments he stood there, just watching the floating debris. And then, he spotted a dead trout in the water, and then a few others. Was there any more sickening sight, he thought sadly, than that of a trout, its white belly pointed skyward? He couldn't think of anything more sickening.

Jack stared out at the stream, taking in the roiling waters. For one final time, he wanted to breathe in the very scent of the stream, to allow it to roll over his very being. He probed the bump near his elbow with his fingers. No. It hadn't grown since he'd first discovered it. Did it matter?

He took off his fishing vest and dropped it on the wet ground and then his fly rod. He debated in his mind whether to get out of his waders. It would, he realized, be better with the waders on. Sure, it would. They would fill up with water and make this so much easier.

He slowly waded into the Shad. His mind swirled with memories of The Shad: the big hatches that gave up bountiful numbers of trout, the evenings with Soothsayer on the stream. Good old wise, patient Soothsayer—his friend, his mentor. And how could he forget that night they had come down here to this very spot to witness the return of the Green Drake Hatch?

He was nearly chest deep in the stream now, the water nearly over his waders. A few more steps, and the water would fill them, and he'd meekly surrender, say good-bye to it all.

Voices came calling to him over the rush of water as he took another step deeper into the stream.

"Jack. Jack. What the hell." Tar was behind him.

Jack raised a single hand above his head. A farewell?

"Jack. N-o-o-o-o-o."

Was that Missy? It didn't matter. Jack took another step, and the water poured into his waders and then the stream knocked him off his feet and the furious current was carrying him away. For a fleeting moment, he felt panic, and then ... nothing really.

"Jack. Jack. Jesus."

He closed his eyes and let the stream take him farther downstream, and soon he was sinking. This was the way to go, he thought.

He was like a trout, that wonderful species of fish, in its natural habitat—in the water, but not just any water—The Shad. And that was a good thing.

The End

The following is an excerpt from Mike Reuther's Pitching for Sanity I.

Chapter 1

There were times when he felt if he didn't throw, he might literally go to pieces. Seven days a week, he would take the bucket of balls and throw them one after the other into the haystack. It was a ritual, but an exercise, a way of exorcising demons, perhaps reliving a dream that had never really taken flight in his youth.

Bill Barrister was a pitcher. That is, he'd been a pitcher back in high school. But no one had taken much notice of his talent back then, save his teammates and the opposing teams that he mowed down with his fastball mixed in with an occasional nasty curveball that some referred to as "the unfair one."

Bill had secrets that he didn't want known. And so, he threw into the haystack. He loved the rhythm of throwing, of the sound the ball made when it smacked into the haystack, of the way his body felt as it unwound.

He didn't realize how much he'd missed just throwing a ball repeatedly, almost like clockwork. All those years when he'd been away, getting through the long days of a career in the Air Force. Working security in lonely outposts overseas and in the states, mostly in Texas.

Texas had been so much of his life for so long. Married and divorced from a Texas woman who couldn't help him. Now, back in Pennsylvania. Why had he come back? He wasn't sure. The one thing he was sure of anymore was this ritual of throwing into the haystack.

He'd found the baseballs in the shed at the back of his boyhood home just two days after serving twenty years in the military. Several dozen of them, brown and grass-stained and well-used, some with the stitching unraveling, were piled like rocks in a rusty bucket. Why had they not been tossed out with all the other remnants of his boyhood by his mom?

Mom had died a few years earlier, leaving him, an only son, this house. Maybe they were kept around to remind her of the game her husband and son so loved. His dad, a semi-pro ballplayer in the 1940s and 1950s, and Bill, a star pitcher of his American Legion teams.

But dad was dead now. Nearly twenty years now, not long after Bill had left home for the Air Force. Killed in an automobile accident out on Highway 17. "Life is full of accidents son," his dad had said. "But luck is the residue of design."

"Which is it?" Bill asked.

"What do you think?" his dad said.

Jean Barrister was a man of few words, and his son had grown into the same kind of laconic man.

His dad had been a home run hitter. Not a big man, he'd been blessed with quicks wrists or good timing or that special combination of body motions that worked in sync to send batted balls flying over outfield fences.

"Your old man wasn't big, but he could hit the shit out of the ball," more than one teammate from his father's playing days had told Bill.

Bill wanted to be a hitter too, but curveballs especially gave him fits. All through his youth he struggled to hit .200. He hated striking out, and once a pitcher got two strikes on him, his only thought was not missing the ball, which too often ended badly.

But it helped him too. When he pitched, he knew many of the hitters feared striking out. He used it to his advantage, knowing he had a psychological edge when he got two strikes on a batter.

"You think too much Bill."

His old man told him that. So did his American Legion coach, a little man named Doc, who hardly appeared fit to sum up the relative merits of ballplayers, or any athletes for that matter. "You got a great arm kid, but you worry."

It was true. Worries swirled in his head. But not just on the ball field. Would he pass eleventh grade? How did he look when he walked down the hallways of his high school? Did girls laugh at him behind his back? Was he a good enough person? Did he deserve to be happy?

Sometimes he prayed, not so much out of religious fervor as a need to protect himself. He didn't really know if there was a God up there somewhere watching him. Playing baseball for Bill meant hopping over baselines, or sitting in the same spot in the dugout where he made sure all the bats were lined just right in a row, or pounding his glove with his right hand exactly five times before he threw. He needed these rituals.

All through his teenage years, his stomach was often tight, his mind filled with "what if thinking." What *if* he couldn't throw strikes. What *if* he obsessed too much about sex? God. Maybe he'd turn into a sex addict. What *if* the world blew up? Could just *thinking* about it make it happen? In his idle moments, his brain just wouldn't stop with these thoughts – a runaway freight train of manic meanderings of the mind.

He'd pace the hallway of his home just outside his bedroom at three in the morning to ward off the thoughts.

It was his mother who finally insisted that he talk to someone about his problems. And so, he did.

"You're a nervous teenager," said the psychologist in a calm reassuring voice. "Nothing unusual. It will pass."

But it didn't pass. The thoughts, the worries, only seemed to get worse. He fought, he wrestled with the thoughts, which only increased his anxieties.

Schoolwork was a nightmare, his focus always elsewhere, all learning eluding him like bad hop groundballs. Only through sheer will did he barely pass his courses every year to make it to the next grade. He couldn't imagine failing, being held back. And yet, he found that worries about his schoolwork canceled out the other worries that often consumed him: Was he good enough? Would the world end? Was he a sex-obsessed teenager? Would he ever be able to throw strikes again?

Chapter 2

"He doesn't have a job."

"What?" said Stevie McNutt.

""I'm tellin' ya," said Robby. "He's doesn't have a job. He's a bum."

"A bum?"

Robby's words stunned Stevie. What was a bum?

"They say he just hangs out in that house all day and drinks."

"But he's not drinking now," said Stevie as they both watched Bill throw another ball at the haystack behind his house.

"That's all he does, said Robby. "Drink and throw baseballs. He's a little crazy."

"Crazy?"

"C'mon," said Robby. "Let's get a little closer. Robby pushed off with his one foot to move his bicycle closer to the curb in front of Bill's house. Stevie stayed back, unsure whether it was a good idea to get any closer. His mother had always warned him about spying on people. It just wasn't a nice thing to do, she said.

"Hey mister," yelled Robby.

Stevie saw Bill stop throwing in mid motion and turn to look at Robby who straddled his bike.

"Let's get out of here," said Stevie. He moved his own bicycle back, his right foot on the pedal, ready to race away if the odd man he knew as Bill came after them.

"Hey mister," yelled Robby. "What are ya tryin' to do? Strike out Barry Bonds?"

Bill stood with the baseball smiling. He shook his head, turned and wound up to throw another ball.

"Hey mister," said Robby. "Can you get us a beer."

Bill said nothing. He threw more balls at the haystack. It was a warm June evening, and he could feel the sweat on his forehead. He'd been out in his yard throwing for the past ten minutes, and it was nearing time to quit.

After a few more throws, he picked up the bucket beside him and carried it down to the haystack where he gathered up the balls scattered about on the ground. He was aware of the kids still out there on Penn Avenue watching him. They had been stopping by on different days throughout the spring and in these early days of summer. Other times, they'd pedaled by on their bikes in the alley behind the garage here at the end of the lot where he had the haystack set up. Screw it. He figured they were just curious kids, wondering who the crazy old guy was tossing baseballs.

When he came walking up the backyard with the balls, he saw that they were gone. He was a bit disappointed about that. He thought he might invite them into the yard, show them a few things - how to throw a curveball, the best grip for a fastball. Then again, it was probably a good idea to keep his distance. You just couldn't talk to kids these days without everyone getting their guard up, thinking you were some kind of child molester or something.

"We saw him again out there tonight," said Stevie to his mother.

Stevie and Robby sat on the front porch of Stevie's home a block away on Salt Street. The house was one of those old

Victorians that had seen its better days, a big three-story home with poor plumbing and in bad need of a paint job. Stevie's mother, Sarah, loved the house, despite its flaws, especially the large porch that wrapped around the front and one side of it where she liked to sit on summer nights. Sarah, a divorcee who sold real estate, had gotten what she thought was a good deal on the house.

"You kids should probably stay away from there." Sarah put the tray with the two glasses of lemonade down on the small metal table sitting in front of the chaise lounge where the two boys sat.

"He was throwing those baseballs at the haystack again," said Stevie.

Sarah stood looking down at her son as she brushed back a strand of hair from her face. She was a pretty woman in her mid-thirties. It had been three years since she'd left her husband, Stevie's father. He was a mechanic, *when* he worked, with big dreams of running his own garage. The problem was he had too many issues to run a business. He drank. He chased women and money ran through his hands like water. "At least he doesn't hit you," said her mom.

"I'm getting out of the marriage," Sarah said. And she did. But not until after she'd picked up the real estate license and gotten a job selling properties. She soon found out it was something she was pretty good at too. She knew how to smile and could be a people person when she wanted, including doing the networking necessary for the job and chatting up people on the phone. And, she was keeping her own household together.

"You didn't put enough sugar in the lemonade mom," said Stevie.

Sarah sighed. "Give me your glass. How about you Robby?"

"It's good Mrs. McNutt."

"Good. I'm batting five hundred."

"Good joke mom."

She plopped down in the chair and looked out on Salt Street. It was just starting to get dark out, and some of the lights were on in the houses along the street. She noticed the yard needed mowed. But that was the least of her problems with this house. She loved the old house, but it was just too big. Since the divorce, she had closed off a couple of the rooms on the second floor to save on heating bills in the winter. The paint beneath her feet on the porch was peeling. One thing about her ex-husband. He had been kind of good about keeping up repairs around the place when he wasn't drinking or out chasing one of his floozies.

"You going to take us to the Little League game tomorrow night mom?" asked Stevie.

"Oh, that's right. You kids have a game. Don't you?"

"We play the Cubs," said Robby. "They're in first place."

"If we beat 'em. We tie them for first place," added Stevie.

"Oh dear," Sarah said. "I'm supposed to show a house tomorrow evening."

"Aw mom, c'mon," said Stevie.

She let out a sigh. "I'll have to see if I can reschedule," she said.

Always something, she thought. It hadn't been easy before the divorce being a kind of Little League mom in this town. Maybe, she thought, she should join one of those single mothers' groups or get on the Internet and see what advice was out there for single moms. God. Had her life really come to that?

"Robby. What time do you have to be home?" she asked. She wanted to get a glass of wine and maybe sit out here on the porch — all by herself. It was one of the few real pleasures in life she seemed to enjoy anymore.

"Aw. I'm okay. My mom says I don't have to be home till at least ten in the summer time."

She nodded. Robby was a bright kid, living in a two-parent family, a rare household, even in this little town of Pearisville, where conservative values still managed to hang on in these crazy times. It seemed like everyone she knew had voted for George Bush and his father.

Stevie looked at his mother. He was a bright kid too, hip to her subtle hints. "C'mon Robby," he said. "I'll show you my new game. The two of them sprang up from the chaise lounge and raced across the front porch, the screen door flying open and yawning shut.

And just like that, Sarah was alone on the front porch. A few more lights had come on in the houses. Some bats were zig-zagging amidst the branches of the elms and maples lining the street. She felt tired. Too tired to get up and get that glass of wine? The phone in her house rang.

"Hello?"

"Mrs. McNutt?" It was a man's voice. It sounded low and husky, but a bit unsure.

"Yes. This is Mrs. McNutt."

"The real estate lady?"

"Yes."

"Is that your son who keeps watching me with his friend?"

"I'm sorry ..."

"I like to throw baseballs."

She didn't know what to say. "Okay ... " was all she could get out.

"Yeah. It is okay. Look ... I don't mind. But your son or that other kid ... not sure which one it was ... got a little mouthy. I'd appreciate it if they don't yell things at me."

Sarah could feel the sweat from her hand gripping the cell phone. "I'm sorry ... what's your name?"

"It's Bill." There was a pause. "Have a nice night."

Made in United States
Orlando, FL
24 May 2023

33449773R00095